D1087569

FORMS OF GOVERNMENT
AND THE
RISE OF DEMOCRACY

Britannica
Educational Publishing

IN ASSOCIATION WITH

ROSEN
EDUCATIONAL SERVICES

FORMS OF GOVERNMENT
AND THE
RISE OF DEMOCRACY

EDITED BY BRIAN DUIGNAN, SENIOR EDITOR, RELIGION AND PHILOSOPHY

Britannica
Educational Publishing

IN ASSOCIATION WITH

ROSEN
EDUCATIONAL SERVICES

321
For

Published in 2013 by Britannica Educational Publishing
(a trademark of Encyclopædia Britannica, Inc.)
in association with Rosen Educational Services, LLC
29 East 21st Street, New York, NY 10010.

Distributed exclusively by Rosen Educational Services.
For a listing of additional Britannica Educational Publishing titles, call toll free (800) 237-9932.

First Edition

Britannica Educational Publishing
J.E. Luebering: Senior Manager
Marilyn L. Barton: Senior Coordinator, Production Control
Steven Bosco: Director, Editorial Technologies
Lisa S. Braucher: Senior Producer and Data Editor
Yvette Charboneau: Senior Copy Editor
Kathy Nakamura: Manager, Media Acquisition
Brian Duignan, Senior Editor, Religion and Philosophy

Pub
5|28

Rosen Educational Services
Jeanne Nagle: Senior Editor
Nelson Sá: Art Director
Cindy Reiman: Photography Manager
Karen Huang: Photo Researcher
Brian Garvey: Designer, Cover Design
Introduction by Brian Duignan

Library of Congress Cataloging-in-Publication Data

Forms of government and the rise of democracy/edited by Brian Duignan.—1st ed.
   p. cm.—(Governance: power, politics, and participation)
Includes bibliographical references and index.
ISBN 978-1-61530-671-8 (library binding)
1. State, The. 2. Political science—History. 3. Comparative government. 4. Democracy. I.
Duignan, Brian.
JC348.F67 2011
321—dc23

                                                              2011045689

Manufactured in the United States of America

CONTENTS

115

118

131

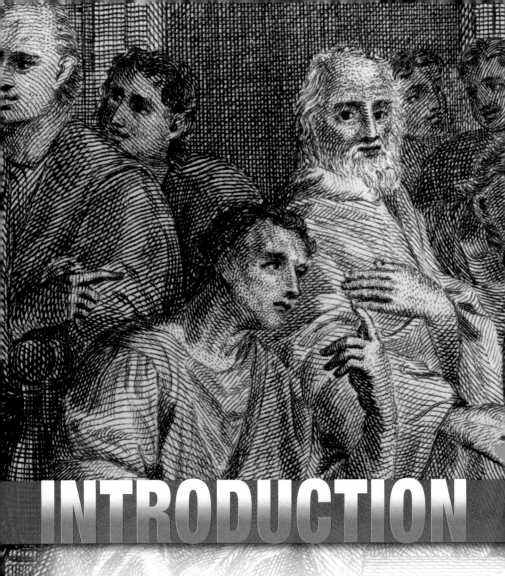

INTRODUCTION

As it is commonly used, the term "government" is ambig-uous, having at least two distinct meanings. In one sense, it may refer to the political leadership of a country, region, state, city, or other political entity—that is, to the individuals or groups within the entity who hold executive power. In another sense, "government" may refer to the for-mal legal institutions, rules, and procedures through which the political leadership and other officials direct or perform the functions of governing, which often are established in a constitution.

Ancient Greek statesman Solon explaining his code of laws to the Athenians. Solon's political reforms helped set the groundwork for modern democracy. Archive Photos/Getty Images

Governments in this sense are sometimes called "political systems," though this terminology technically has a broader meaning. A political system refers not only to formal elements of government, but also to various informal or unofficial structures and processes, together with the ways in which both formal and informal elements influence, and are influenced by, the political entity's economy, society, and culture.

In this book, which concerns the history of government and the rise of democracy in the West, the term "government" is used most often in the second sense of the term. This survey of the development of government from ancient times to the present will prove a rewarding resource for anyone interested in the history and future of democratic government.

As a political system, the government of the United States is constituted by three branches—the executive, the legislative, and the judicial, each with its own constitutionally prescribed functions and powers. Each branch also exists on two levels—the federal, or U.S., government and the state government, the latter of which possess all the powers "not delegated to the United States by the Constitution, nor prohibited by it to the States," according to the Tenth Amendment (1791). A form of government, accordingly, is a way to classify individual governments by the various formal elements they have in common. Both the United States and the United Kingdom, for example, have democratic forms of government, because both have institutions and procedures for regularly electing the country's political leadership. However, whereas the United States has a federal system, in which power is constitutionally divided between a central level of government and one or more lower levels, the United Kingdom has a unitary system, in which all power is held or delegated by the central level.

Governments first emerged in the ancient land of Sumer, between the Tigris and Euphrates rivers in what is now Iraq. The gradual development of agriculture on a large scale in Sumerian societies required an increasingly complex division of labor between various groups (e.g., farmers, engineers, warriors, priests, scribes, and tax collectors), many of which were characterized by the possession of specialized skills and knowledge. An elaborate division of labor in turn depended on an established system of political authority for organizing and directing the work of thousands of individuals at different levels. The governments of such societies were typically monarchical, being ruled by a single individual. Eventually, as their populations and territories grew—and particularly as successful societies expanded by conquering others—the monarch's ultimate authority would be exercised through numerous lower-level officials, who might be responsible for supervising certain governmental functions or ruling particular geographic areas within the monarch's realm. Monarchy was the form of government of many of the great civilizations of the ancient world, including that of Babylonia, China, Israel, Egypt, India, Persia, and imperial Rome. It continued to be the most common form of government in the West until approximately the late 18th century.

Democracy as a form of government was invented and perfected in ancient Athens some 2,500 years ago. Ancient Greece was not a single political entity but a collection of hundreds of independent poleis, or city-states (i.e., states whose formal territory consists entirely of a city and its surrounding countryside). Among them was Athens, whose relatively small population made it possible to govern the city through votes taken at regular meetings of the popular Assembly. Any any eligible voter could attend these meetings (though in practice not all did). Other Greek city-states exhibited different forms of government, including monarchy, aristocracy, oligarchy, and tyranny—the last defined by Aristotle as rule by a single individual in his own interest, rather than in the interest of everyone.

Athens remained independent and fully democratic almost continuously until 338 BCE, when it was conquered by Philip II of Macedonia. Philip's famous son, Alexander the Great, significantly expanded his father's conquests, establishing a short-lived empire that stretched from the western Mediterranean, including Greece and Egypt, through Persia (modern-day Iran) to northwestern India. Upon Alexander's premature death in 323, his generals became monarchs of the several separate states into which they divided his territories.

The Mediterranean kingdoms of the Hellenistic Age were eventually conquered by Rome, itself originally a city-state. At their largest extent the territories ruled by the Romans included the British Isles, all of the western European continent, North Africa, the Balkans, and the entire eastern Mediterranean, including much of what is today called the Middle East. During the first 500 years of its existence the Roman republic, as the Romans called it ("republic" is derived from *res publica*, or "the thing that belongs to the people"), was a unique and complex mixture of aristocracy and democracy that incorporated no less than five assemblies, foremost among them the Senate. In the late 1st century BCE, Rome descended into a series of civil wars between the armies of ambitious generals, in part because it had become so large. The eventual victor, Octavian, became the Roman emperor Augustus and established the empire's particular form of government, the "principate," which combined monarchy with some elements of the former republic, including the aristocratic Senate. The emperor's powers were essentially absolute, however, and after their deaths all emperors were worshipped as gods.

The Roman empire was permanently divided into western and eastern halves in 395 CE. In the 5th century the western half was overrun by Germanic tribes, though the basic institutions of imperial government were initially preserved. The eastern empire, from this time known as the Byzantine Empire, survived until 1453, when it finally succumbed to the Ottoman Turks.

After the disintegration of Roman rule, western Europe split apart into myriad and constantly warring tribal kingdoms. The powers of the kings, however, were greatly limited, because they relied on a large landed aristocracy for income and arms. The feudal system, as it is now called, continued for some 400 years before gradually declining as increased trade and the growth of cities reduced the economic importance of landed estates. Kings and princes became less dependent on the aristocracy and were slowly able to consolidate their power over increasingly larger territories.

By about 1500 a new political entity, the nation-state, had emerged in England, France, and Spain. The form of government by which it was ruled, the monarchy, was not new, though new institutions, including large royal bureaucracies, had been established to assist monarchs in the exercise of their enormous powers. Because of the great extent of these powers, which lasted until the late 18th century, this period is commonly designated as "the age of absolutism."

It should be emphasized, however, that the powers of absolute monarchs varied between countries and generations. The monarchy in England, for example, was increasingly circumscribed by Parliament. During the English Civil Wars (1642–51), parliamentary forces overthrew and executed King James I and established a short-lived republican government. Under the terms of the restoration of the monarchy in 1689, Parliament retained significant powers, including the power to lay taxes. England thus became the first constitutional monarchy, a form of government in which power is divided by constitutional prescription between the monarch and other institutions or offices. The United Kingdom is still a constitutional monarchy, though the monarch's role is now purely ceremonial.

During the 18th and 19th centuries the government of Britain gradually became more democratic as the monarch ceded more powers to Parliament and as Parliament itself became more representative of the British population, in part through a painfully slow expansion of the franchise in the various Reform Acts. As a result of these transformations Britain became a representative democracy, a form of government in which elected representatives determine government policy according to the wishes of the people. This policy is made known indirectly through the platforms of the representatives who win election.

Representative democracy thus contrasts with the direct democracy of Athens, in which the people themselves determined government policy by a direct show of hands. Partly because it requires a venue large enough to stage simultaneous votes by all citizens, direct democracy was thought to be impossible in political entities larger than a town or small city. The creation of large representative institutions, such as the U.S. Congress, was thus the key to extending democracy beyond the city-state to provinces, regions, and nation-states, as the Founding Fathers of the United States well knew.

The United States is the oldest continuously existing democracy in the world. However, the U.S. Constitution placed limits on democracy by ensuring that a majority of citizens could never vote to take away the fundamental rights of a minority. Among the rights protected in the first 10 amendments to the Constitution, known collectively as the Bill of Rights, are the freedoms of speech, religion, and the press; the right against unreasonable searches and seizures (the right to privacy); and the right against cruel and unusual punishment. The French Declaration of the Rights of Man and of the Citizen, adopted after the French Revolution in 1789, also established guarantees against democratic tyranny. These documents express what is now a universal consensus, that democracy is not equivalent merely to the rule of a majority. In order to be fully democratic, governments must also protect the basic rights of their citizens.

During the 20th century, Western democracy was nearly extinguished by the forces of fascism, and it was endangered for several decades by Soviet communism. In the late 20th and early 21st centuries, new threats to democracy emerged, including some that originated within the democracies themselves. The growing inequality of wealth between the industrialized and developing worlds, and between the rich and the poor in many countries, tended to convince those who were suffering that democracy did not help them and that more radical solutions were required. (This very sentiment enabled the Nazis to gain representation in the German Reichstag starting in the late 1920s.) Similarly, the spread of terrorism since the 1990s convinced many people that some of the basic rights underlying democratic government, such as the rights to free speech and privacy, must be curtailed in order to increase the powers of police and intelligence agencies to protect national security. It should be noted that this was not the first time that democratic freedoms and national security were thought to be incompatible.

For most of human history democracy did not exist. Indeed, it did not become a common form of government until the mid-20th century. Perhaps for that reason it should not be assumed that democracies will continue to be common in the years to come. Nor is it clear what particular forms future democracies may take. For instance, advanced communications technologies may one day make it possible for all citizens to vote frequently and simultaneously, thereby moving democratic governments closer to direct democracy. As with all forms of government, democracy can, and most likely will, change with the times.

CHAPTER 1

Primitive Government to the End of the Middle Ages

The term *government* refers to the set of formal legal institutions, rules, and procedures by which a country or community is administered and regulated. Most of the key words commonly used to describe forms of government—such as *monarchy*, *oligarchy*, and *democracy*—are of Greek or Roman origin. They have been current for more than 2,000 years and have not yet exhausted their usefulness. This suggests that humankind has not altered very much since they were coined. However, such verbal and psychological uniformity must not be allowed to hide the enormous changes in society and politics that have occurred.

The earliest analytical use of the term *monarchy* occurred in ancient Athens, in the dialogues of Plato (*c.* 428–*c.* 348 BCE), but even in Plato's time the term was not self-explanatory. There was a king in Macedonia and a king in Persia, but the two societies, and therefore their institutions, were radically different. To give real meaning to the word *monarchy* in those two instances, it would be necessary to investigate their actual political and historical contexts. Any general account of monarchy required then, and requires today, an inquiry as to what circumstances have predisposed societies to adopt monarchy and what have led them to reject it. So it is with *oligarchy, democracy,* and all other political terms.

PRIMITIVE GOVERNMENT

So long as humans were few, there was hardly any government. The division of function between ruler and ruled occurred only, if at all, within the family. The largest social groups, whether tribes or villages, were little more than loose associations of families, in which every elder or family head had an equal voice. Chieftains, if any, had strictly limited powers; some tribes did without chieftains altogether. This prepolitical form of social organization may still be found in some regions of the world, such as parts of the Amazonian jungle in South America or the Upper Nile Valley in Africa.

AGRICULTURAL SOCIETY

The rise of agriculture began to change that state of affairs. In the land of Sumer (in what is now Iraq) the invention of irrigation necessitated grander arrangements. Control of the flow of water down the Tigris and Euphrates rivers had to be coordinated by a central authority, so that fields could be watered downstream as well as farther up. It became necessary also to devise a calendar, so as to know when the spring floods might be expected. As those skills evolved, society evolved with them. In early Sumer, it is reasonable to assume, the heads of the first cities, which were little more than enlarged villages, only gradually assumed the special attributes of monarchy—the rule of one—and the village council only gradually undertook a division of labour, so that some specialized as priests and others as warriors, farmers, or tax gatherers (key figures in every civilized society). As organization grew more complex, so did religion: an elaborate system of worship seemed necessary to propitiate the quite elaborate family of gods who, it was hoped, would protect the city from attack, from natural disaster, and from any questioning of the political arrangements deemed necessary by the ruler group.

Unfortunately—but, given human nature, inevitably—the young cities of Sumer quarrelled over the distribution

A Brazilian Amazon chief waits to greet members of the British royal family in 2009. Early tribal chieftains led primitive governments, albeit often with limited authority. WPA Pool/Getty Images

of the rivers' water, and their wealth excited the greed of nomads outside the still comparatively small area of *civilization* (a word deriving from the Latin word for city, *civitas*). War, perhaps the most potent of all forces of historical change, announced its arrival, and military leadership became at least as important an element of kingship as divine sanction. It was to remain so throughout the long history of monarchy: whenever kings have neglected their military duties, they have endangered their thrones. The wars of Sumer also laid bare another imperative of monarchy—the drive for empire, arising from the need to defend and define frontiers by extending them and the need to find new means to pay for troops and weapons, whether by the plunder of an enemy or by the conquest of new lands, or both.

THE SPREAD OF CIVILIZATION

The history of Old World monarchy, and indeed of civilization, was to consist largely of variations on the patterns mentioned above for four or five millennia. Trade contacts carried the principles of civilization to Egypt and to India (China, like the pre-Columbian societies of the Americas, seems to have evolved independently); and everywhere, once the social order was established, the problem of defending it became paramount. For although the broad zone of civilization spread steadily, so that by the reign of the Roman emperor Trajan (98–117 CE) there was a continuous band of civilized societies from Britain to the China Sea, it was always at risk from the barbarian nomads who roamed the great steppelands of central Eurasia. These nomads had retained the loose and simple institutions of primitive societies, but they had in other ways evolved as rapidly and successfully as the cities themselves (and partly under the cities' influence). The steppe was horse

4

country, and, armed with bows and arrows, the barbarians of all epochs were marvelously swift and deadly with light cavalry. They fought constantly among themselves for pasturage, and the losers were forever being driven west, south, and east, where they often overcame any defenses that the farms and cities of civilization could muster against them.

Yet the nomads' military challenge was never sufficient to overturn civilization entirely. Either the invaders would overrun the settled lands and then adopt civilized customs, or the frontier defenses would prove strong enough to hold them off. There were even long periods of peace, when the barbarian threat was negligible. It was at such times that the spontaneous ingenuity of humankind had greatest play, in politics as in everything else. But it is noteworthy that, in the end, what may be described as the ancient norm always reasserted itself, whether in Europe, the Middle East, India, or China. Military crises—barbarian invasions, civil wars, or war between competing polities—recurred, necessitating the strengthening of government.

The effort to secure a measure of peace and prosperity required the assertion of authority over vast distances, the raising of large armies, and the gathering of taxes to pay for them. Those requirements in turn fostered literacy and numeracy and the emergence of what later came to be called bureaucracy—government by officials. Bureaucratic imperialism emerged again and again and spread with civilization. Barbarian challenge occasionally laid it low but never for very long. When one city or people rose to hegemony over its neighbours, it simply incorporated their bureaucracy into its own. Sumer and Babylon were conquered by Assyria; Assyria was overthrown by the Medes of Persia, in alliance with a resurgent Babylon and nomadic Scythians; the empire of the Persians was overthrown by Alexander the Great (356–323 BCE) of Macedonia; the Macedonian successor states were conquered by Rome, which was in due course supplanted in the Middle East and North Africa by the Islamic Caliphate of Baghdad. Conquerors came and went, but life for their subjects, whether peasants or towns-people, was not much altered by anything they did, as long as the battles happened elsewhere.

Nevertheless, from time to time experiments were made, for no monarchy had the resources to rule all its subjects directly. So long as they paid tribute punctually, local rulers and local communities were perforce left to govern themselves. Even if they did not pay, the effort required to mount a military operation at a distance from the imperial centre was so great that only in exceptional circumstances would it be undertaken, and even then it might not succeed, as the kings of Persia found when they launched punitive expeditions from Asia Minor against mainland Greece at the beginning of the 5th century BCE. Thus, in normal times the inhabitants of the borderlands had extensive freedom of action.

Although civilization, as its advantages became clear, spread west and northwest out of Asia, bureaucratic monarchy could not easily follow it. The sea was becoming a historical factor as important as the steppe and the great irrigable rivers. Tyre and Sidon, maritime cities of Phoenicia (modern Lebanon), had long exploited their coastal situation, not only to remain independent of the landward empires but also to push across the sea, even beyond the Straits of Gibraltar, in quest of trade. Their daughter-cities, Carthage, Utica, and Cádiz, were the first colonies, but primitive communications made it impossible for Phoenicia to rule them.

CLASSICAL GREECE

The Phoenician example was followed by the Greeks, originally Indo-European nomads who gradually made their way south to the Aegean and there took to the sea.

THE MINOANS

The Minoans were a non-Indo-European people who flourished from about 3000 to about 1100 BCE on the island of Crete during the Bronze Age. The sea was the basis of their economy and power. Their sophisticated culture, based at Knossos, was named for the legendary King Minos. It represented the first high civilization in the Aegean area. The Minoans exerted great influence on the Mycenaean culture of the Greek islands and mainland. Minoan culture reached its peak *c.* 1600 BCE and was noted for its cities and palaces, extended trade contacts, and use of writing. Its art included elaborate seals, pottery, and, notably, the vibrant frescoes decorating palace walls, which depicted both religious and secular scenes, including goddesses reflective of a matriarchal religion. Palace ruins show evidence of paved streets and piped water. Familiar Minoan art motifs are the snake (symbol of the goddess) and the bull and leaping dancer, also of mystical significance.

They built on the achievements of earlier peoples and even took over the first bureaucratic monarchy to appear on European soil, the Minoan civilization of the island of Crete, which succumbed to invaders from the Greek mainland in about 1450 BCE. Other invaders from the north overthrew the mainland kingdoms of Mycenae, Tiryns, and Pylos in about 1200 BCE.

THE CITY-STATE

The so-called dark ages of Greece that then began lasted until the 8th century BCE, by which time the Greeks not only had adapted the Phoenician alphabet and begun to found overseas colonies but also had brought nearly to maturity the city-state (*polis* in Greek, from which the term *politics* derives). This form of government was the great political invention of classical antiquity.

The city-state was made possible by Mediterranean geography, which is such that every little fishing village had to be able to defend itself against attack from land or sea, for outside help could not reach it easily. A person's dependence on his community, for physical as well as economic survival, was therefore obvious and complete. The city had first claim on his labour and loyalty, a claim that was usually freely recognized. It was this reality that led Aristotle (who himself came from just such a small commonwealth, Stageira) to define man as a political animal. In addition, coastal mountain ranges made it difficult for any community in Greece to dominate more than a few square miles of land. Therefore, in the Greek world (which by *c.* 600 BCE stretched from the coasts of Asia Minor to what is now southern France), there were dozens of centres of government. The term *city-state* expresses the double aspect of those small settlements.

Each city-state was, on the one hand, an economic, cultural, and religious organization; on the other hand, each was a self-governing community capable, in theory, of maintaining absolute independence by enlisting all its adult male inhabitants as soldiers. It was like a business association and also like an encamped army. (In many respects, the city of Sparta actually was an encamped army.) Freedom was defined as the right and ability of every city to govern itself. What freedom meant for the internal order of such cities was fiercely and often bloodily debated for more than two centuries.

Although it was a fact of the Greek world that geography deterred the rise of an empire to federate and control all the cities, a few nevertheless rose to imperial greatness. Those cities engaged in profitable trade across the sea, as

8

their Phoenician predecessors had done. Athens, for example, exported olive oil, silver, and pottery, and the profits of that trade enabled it to build a great navy and formidable city walls. Athenian ships defeated Persia (480 BCE) and won a small empire in the Aegean; the combination of ships and walls enabled Athens long to defy and nearly to defeat Sparta, its chief rival among the Greek cities. Even after Sparta's triumph at the end of the Peloponnesian War (404 BCE), Athens remained an independent, sovereign state until its defeat by Philip II of Macedonia at the battle of Chaeronea (338 BCE). In short, during the period of its prime Athens was free to make what experiments it liked in the realm of government, and to that period are owed not just the first example of successful democracy in world history but also the first investigations in political thought.

MONARCHY, OLIGARCHY, DEMOCRACY

No Athenian believed that he had anything to learn from the bureaucratic monarchies of the East, which were incompatible with Greek notions of citizenship. If self-defense necessitated that every citizen be required to fight for his polis when called on, in return each had to be conceded some measure of respect and autonomy—personal freedom. To protect that freedom, government was necessary: anarchy had no attractions for any Greek except perhaps Diogenes, the father of Cynic philosophy.

The central question of politics, then, was the distribution of power among the citizens. Was Greek freedom best preserved and defined by the rule of the few or by that of the many? On the whole, the great names favoured aristocracy—the rule of the best. Plato believed that the object of politics was virtue, and that only a few would ever thoroughly understand the science by which virtue

9

could be attained and that those trained few should rule. Aristotle, his pupil, seems to have put the cultivation of the intellect highest among human goods, and he believed—quite reasonably, given the limited economic resources then available—that this fruit of civilization could be gathered only among a leisured class supported by the labours of the many. In return for their leisure, the gentry should agree to sacrifice some of their time to the tedious business of governing, which only they would be sufficiently disinterested and well-informed to do successfully. Neither of these apologies for oligarchy had any success in practice. The champions of democracy carried the day, at least in Athens and its allied cities. In return for playing their parts as soldiers or sailors, ordinary Athenians insisted on controlling the government.

The result was imperfect but impressive. The people were misled by demagogues; they were intolerant enough to put Plato's master, Socrates, to death; they were envious of all personal distinction; and of their three great wars (against Persia, Sparta, and Macedonia), they lost two. Furthermore, passionate devotion to the idea that Athens was the greatest of all cities, the school of Greece and the wonder of civilization, misled them into basing their society in large part on slave labour, into wanton imperial adventure abroad, and into denying Athenian citizenship to all who were not born into it (even Aristotle), however much they contributed to the city's greatness and however much more they might have done. The foundations of Athenian democracy were narrow, shallow, and fragile. But to say all this is only to say that the city could not entirely shake off the traditions of its past. Its achievement was the more remarkable for that. Seldom since has civilized humanity surpassed democratic Athens, and until the last the city was satisfactorily governed by law and by popular decision. It owed its fall less to any flaw than to the overwhelming force that was mounted against it.

For to the north of Hellas proper, a new power arose. Greek civilization had slowly trained and tamed the wild men of Macedonia. Their king, Philip II, forged them into a powerful army; he and his son Alexander the Great then seized the opportunity open to them. History and geography made it impossible for the Greek cities to hang together, so they were hanged separately. It seemed as if the city-state had been but a transient expedient. Henceforward Athens and Sparta would take their orders from foreign conquerors—first Macedonia, then Rome.

ROME

But, as it turned out, the city-state had barely begun to display its full political potential. To the west, two non-Greek cities, Carthage and Rome, began to struggle for mastery, and after the defeat of the Carthaginian general Hannibal at Zama (202 BCE), Rome emerged as the strongest state in the Mediterranean.

THE ROMAN REPUBLIC

The Greeks did not know how to classify Rome. The Greek historian Polybius, who chronicled Rome's rise, suggested that its constitution was such a success because it was a judicious blend of monarchy, aristocracy, and democracy. The Romans, a conservative, practical people, showed what they thought of such abstractions by speaking only of an unanalyzed "public thing"—*rēspūblica*—and thus gave a new word, *republic*, to politics. With this focus the patriotism of the city-state reached its greatest intensity. The Romans were deeply attached to their traditions, all of which taught the same lesson. For example, the legendary hero Gaius Mucius Scaevola gave his right hand to the flames to prove that there was nothing a Roman would not endure for his city, which therefore would never be defeated. That passionate devotion to Rome's survival was tested again and again in war. All the tales of early Rome turn on battle. With dour persistence the peasants who had gathered on the seven hills beside the Tiber river resisted every invader, fought back after every defeat, learned from all their mistakes, and even, however reluctantly and belatedly, modified their political institutions to meet the new needs of the times as they arose.

Polybius was right: power in Rome was indeed shared among the people, the aristocracy (embodied in the Senate), and the consuls—the executive officers of the republic who had replaced the kings. The claims of the many and the few were fought out at election time, when the world's first clearly identifiable political parties appeared. Until the republic's decline, the results of elections were universally respected, and the triumphant alliance of the few and the many against the world was proclaimed in the letters blazoned on the city's buildings and battle standards: "SPQR," for *Senatus populusque Romanus* ("The Senate and the people of Rome").

Like Athenian democracy, this system worked well for a long time, and if the chief Athenian legacy was the proof that politics could be understood and debated logically and that under the right conditions democracy could work, Rome proved that the political process of competition for office and the public discussion of policy were valuable things in themselves.

Nevertheless, the Roman Republic had been forged in a grim world. Wars, always supposedly in self-defense, had gradually extended Rome's power over Italy. It is not surprising that what impressed the world most about the city was its military strength rather than its political institutions, even though the two were intimately related. As the weakness of Rome's neighbours became apparent, the Romans began to believe in their mission to rule, "to spare the conquered and war down the proud," as their greatest poet, Virgil, put it. Military strength, in short, led to military adventurism. By the 1st century BCE, Rome, having become a naval power as well as a military one, had conquered the whole Mediterranean basin and much of its hinterland. The strains of empire building made themselves felt. The Roman armies, no longer composed of citizens temporarily absent from the plow or the workshop but of lifetime professionals, were now loyal to their generals rather than to the state; and those generals brought on civil war as they competed to turn their foreign conquests into power at home. The population of Rome swelled, but economic growth could not keep pace, so many citizens became paupers dependent on a public dole. The aristocrats appointed to govern the provinces saw their postings chiefly as opportunities to get rich quickly by pillaging their unfortunate subjects. The republic could not solve those and other problems and was in the end superseded by the monarchy of Augustus.

THE ROMAN EMPIRE

The bedrock of the emperor Augustus's power was his command of the legions with which he had defeated all his rivals, but he was a much better politician than he was a general, and he knew that naked political power is as insecure as it is expensive. He reduced the military establishment as much as was prudent, laboured to turn the revolutionary faction that had supported his bid for power into a respectable new ruling class, and proclaimed the restoration of the republic in 27 BCE. But not even Augustus could make the restoration real.

The safety of the state, questions of war and peace, and most of the business of governing the empire were now in the hands of a monarch; consequently, there was not enough for the Senate to do, and Augustus never went so far as to restore genuinely free elections or the organs of popular government. He kept the population of the city happy with chariot races, gladiatorial contests, and the dole of bread. Nevertheless, he could not give up the attempt to legitimize his regime. Like earlier monarchs elsewhere, he called in the aid of religion, even though the religion of Rome was as republican as its constitution. Later emperors made their own divinity a tenet of the public faith; later still, they imposed Christianity as the sole legitimate and official religion of the empire, and they exploited the power and prestige of the church to buttress their own authority.

For four centuries the resemblance between Rome and the bureaucratic Eastern monarchies steadily increased. Roman nationalism, Roman traditionalism,

Statue of Caesar Augustus standing watch in Rome. Some scholars believe Augustus' political career outshone his military service. Shutterstock.com

and Roman law survived as legacies that posterity would one day claim, and if nobody much believed in the constitutional shams of Augustus's day, the example of his constitutional monarchy was to prove potent at a much later period.

The age of the city-state was at last drawing to a close. The emperor Caracalla extended Roman citizenship to all subjects of the empire, so that he could tax them more heavily. The demands of the imperial administration began to bankrupt the cities, which had previously prospered as the local organs of government under Rome. New barbarian attacks threw the empire onto the defensive, and in 410 CE the city of Rome itself was captured and sacked by the Visigoths. About 65 years later the last Roman emperor in the West was deposed: henceforward the caesars reigned only in Constantinople and the East.

THE MIDDLE AGES

Seen against the background of the millennia, the fall of the Roman Empire was so commonplace an event that it is almost surprising that so much ink has been spilled in the attempt to explain it. The Visigoths were merely one among the peoples who had been dislodged from the steppe in the usual fashion. They and others, unable to crack the defenses of Sasanian Persia or of the Roman Empire in the East (though it was a near thing), probed farther west and at length found the point of weakness they were seeking on the Alps and the Rhine.

DISSOLUTION AND INSTABILITY

What really needs explaining is the fact that the Western Empire was never restored. Elsewhere, imperial thrones were never vacant for long. Thus in China, after every time of troubles, a new dynasty received "the mandate of Heaven," and a new emperor, or "Son of Heaven," rebuilt order. For instance, in 304 CE the nomadic Huns invaded China, and a long period of disruption followed, but at the beginning of the 7th century the Tang dynasty took charge and began 300 years of rule. Similar patterns mark the history of India and Japan.

The Europeans failed to emulate that story. Justinian I, the greatest of the Eastern Roman (Byzantine) emperors, reconquered large portions of the West in the 6th century, though the destruction wreaked by his soldiers made things worse rather than better. In 800 Charlemagne, king of the Franks, was actually crowned emperor of the Romans by the pope. In later centuries the Hohenstaufen and Habsburg dynasties tried to restore the empire; as late as the 19th century, so did Napoleon I. None of those attempts succeeded. Probably the chance was only real in the earliest period, before western Europe had become used to doing without an overlord. But at that time there was never enough breathing space for society to regain its stability and strength. Most of the barbarian kingdoms, successor states to Rome, succumbed to later assailants. Britain fell away from the empire in the 5th century; the little kingdoms of the Angles and Saxons were just coming together as one kingdom, England, when the Viking invasions began. In the 7th century the Arabs conquered North Africa; in the 8th they took Spain and invaded Gaul. Lombards, Avars, Slavs, Bulgars, and Magyars poured into Europe from the East. Not until German king Otto I's victory over the Magyars at Lechfeld in 955 did those incursions cease, and not until the late 11th century was Latin Christendom more or less secure within its borders; and by then it had been without an effective emperor for more than 600 years.

FEUDALISM

Various institutions had emerged to fill the gap. The Christian church, against enormous odds, had kept the light of religion and learning alive and spread what was left of Roman civilization into Ireland, England, central Europe, and Scandinavia. It also provided a reservoir of literacy against the day when professional government should again be possible. The kings of the barbarians, of whom Charlemagne was the greatest, had provided military leadership and tried to acquire some of the prestige and governmental machinery of the Roman emperors. But the troublous times, during which trade and urban life were minimal, meant that effective power lay with those who controlled the land and its products: a military aristocracy of great estates and fiefs (Latin: *feodum*, hence "feudal system"). The aristocrats called themselves *nobiles* in the Roman fashion and appropriated various late-imperial titles, such as *comes* (count) and *dux* (duke). But those titles were mere decoration. The new kings, lacking the machinery for imperial taxation, could not pay for standing armies. Besides, this was the age in which the heavily armoured cavalryman (*chevalier* in French, *knight* in English) dominated war. He was an autonomous force and thus a much less dependable instrument than a Roman legionary had been. Legally, the new masters of the soil were liegemen of the various kings and princes (it was a maxim that every man had a lord), but in practice they could usually ignore royal claims if they chose. Europe thus fell under the rule of armoured knights, and the course of the next few hundred years gives reason to think that the democrats of Greece were right to distrust the very idea of oligarchy, for the keynote of noble rule seemed to be almost incessant warfare.

THE RISE OF LAW AND THE NATION-STATE

Yet even at their height the military aristocrats never had it all their own way. Strong monarchies gradually developed in England, France, and, a little later, in the Iberian Peninsula. During the most vigorous period of the papacy (*c.* 1050–1300) the Roman Catholic Church was able to modify, if not control, baronial behaviour. Trade gradually revived and brought with it a revitalization not only of the city but also of the city-state in Italy, the Rhineland, and the Low Countries, for the newly prosperous burghers could now afford to build stout walls around their towns, and it was difficult for the nobility to muster sufficient force to besiege them success-fully. Even the peasants from time to time made themselves felt in bloody uprisings, and the nobility itself was far from being a homogeneous or united class.

Medieval Europe, in fact, was a constantly shifting kaleidoscope of political arrangements; to the extent that it ever settled down, it did so on the principle that because everybody's claim to power and property was fragile and inconsistent with everybody else's, a certain degree of mutual forbearance was necessary. This explains the great impor-tance attached to custom, or (as it was called in England) common law. Disputes were still often settled by force, especially when kings were the disputants, but the medieval European became almost as fond of law as of battle. Every great estate was hung about with quasi-permanent lawsuits over ownership of land and the rights and privileges that went with it, and the centralization of the church on the papal court at Rome ensured yet more work for lawyers, the greatest of whom began to merge with the military nobility into an aristocracy of a new kind. Rights, titles, and privi-leges were forever being granted, revoked, and reaffirmed. Parchment deeds (of which Magna Carta, exacted from King John of England by his subjects in 1215, was perhaps the most

An early copy of the Magna Carta, being auctioned off at Sotheby's in 2007. The Magna Carta was a charter of liberties granted by King John of England in 1215. Stephen Chernin/Getty Images

famous) came to regulate political, social, and economic relationships at least as much as the sword did. In those ways the idea of the rule of law was reborn. By the beginning of the early modern period legally demonstrable privileges had become the universal cement of European society. The weak were thus enabled to survive alongside the strong, as everyone in Europe knew to which order of society he belonged.

However, there was a dynamism in European society that prevented it from setting permanently into any pattern. The evolving Europe of privileged orders was also the Europe of rising monarchies. With many setbacks the kings clawed power to themselves; by 1500 most of them presided over bureaucracies (initially staffed by clerics) that would have impressed any Roman emperor. But universal empire was still impossible. The foundations of the new monarchies were purely territorial. The kings of England, France, and Spain had enough to do to enforce their authority within the lands they had inherited or seized and to hammer their realms into some sort of uniformity. That impulse explains the wars of the English against the Welsh, Scots, and Irish; the drive of the French kings toward the Alps, the Pyrenees, and the Rhine; and the rigour of the Spanish kings in forcing Catholicism on their Jewish and Moorish subjects. Uniformity paved the way for the most characteristic governmental form of the modern world, the nation-state.

This entity, like the city-state that it superseded, had and has a double aspect. A nation or people can exist without taking the form of a state: physical geography, economic interest, language, religion, and history, all together or in ones and twos, can create a generally accepted and recognized identity without a political organization. But such an identity can, in the right circumstances, provide a solid foundation for government, and the territorial monarchies' quest for external aggrandizement and administrative uniformity soon began, half deliberately, to exploit that possibility.

CHAPTER 2

Early Modern Government to the End of the 19th Century

The development of the nation-state was not easy, for the monarchs or anyone else. The legacy of the Middle Ages was so intractable that the emergence of nation-states was very slow. It may be argued, however, that the modern period was born during the reign of Henry VIII of England (1509–47), when that king more or less simultaneously declared himself head of the national church and his realm an empire—sovereign and unanswerable to any foreign potentate, particularly the pope.

THE RISE AND FALL OF ABSOLUTE MONARCHY

The rise in power of Henry VIII and other early modern kings may be attributed in part to the use of gunpowder, which had enabled the kings to overbear their turbulent nobles—cannons were extremely effective at demolishing the castles in which rebellious barons had formerly been quite safe. But artillery was exceedingly expensive. A sufficient revenue had always been one of the chief necessities of monarchy, but none of the great European kingdoms, in their autocratic phase, ever succeeded in securing one permanently. The complexities of medieval society had permitted very little coercion of taxpayers. For the rest, money could only be secured by chicanery; by selling offices or crown lands (at the price of a long-term weakening of the monarch); by robbing the church; by a lucky chance, such as the acquisition of the gold and silver of

Mexico and Peru by the king of Spain; or by dealing, on a semi-equal footing, with parliaments (or estates, as they were most generally known).

Yet the monarchs did all they could to resist the rise of such representative institutions—except in England, where Henry VIII and the other Tudor monarchs worked with Parliament to make laws and where the folly of the Stuart kings ultimately ensured Parliament's supremacy. On the whole, however, the monarchs of Europe—especially in France, Spain, Prussia, and Austria—had great success at ruling autocratically. Their style of rule, known as absolute monarchy, or absolutism, was a system in which the monarch was supposed to be supreme, in both lawmaking and policy making; in practice, it was really a system of perpetual negotiation between the king and his most powerful subjects that could not, in the long run, meet the challenges of modern war and social change.

Absolutism lasted into the 18th century. Well before that time, though, three great occurrences— the Renaissance, the Reformation, and the

Henry VIII, oil on panel by the studio of Hans Holbein the Younger, after 1537; in the Walker Art Gallery, Liverpool, Eng. The Bridgeman Art Library/National Museums and Galleries on Merseyside (Walker Art Gallery, Liverpool)

discovery of the Americas—had transformed Europe. Those events contributed to the eventual failure of absolute monarchy and profoundly influenced the development of future governments.

The impact of the Renaissance defies summary, even if its political consequences are all that need be considered. The truest symbol of its importance is the printing press. For one thing, this invention enormously increased the resources of government. Laws, for instance, could be circulated far more widely and more accurately than ever before. More important still was the fact that the printing press increased the size of the educated and literate classes. Renaissance civilization thus became something unprecedented: it acquired deeper foundations than any of its predecessors or contemporaries on any continent by calling into play the intelligence of more individuals than ever before. But the catch (from a ruler's point of view) was that this development also brought public opinion into being for the first time. Not for much longer would it be enough for kings to win the acquiescence of their nobles and the upper clergy; a new force was at work, as was acknowledged by the frantic attempts of all the monarchies to control and censor the press.

The Reformation was the eldest child of the press; it, too, had diffuse and innumerable consequences, the most important of which was the destruction of the Roman Catholic Church's effective claim to universality. It had always been a somewhat fraudulent assertion—the pope's claim to supreme authority had never been accepted by all the Christian bodies, particularly the Orthodox churches of the Greeks and Slavs—but after Martin Luther and John Calvin, the scope of his commands was radically reduced. In the long run, the consequence was the secularization of politics and administration and the introduction of some measure of religious toleration. Gradually the way became clear for rational, utilitarian considerations to shape government.

The discovery of the Americas opened a new epoch in world history. The Spanish overthrew the monarchies of the Aztec and the Inca, thanks partly to the Spaniards' superior weapons and partly to the diseases they brought with them. It was a spectacular episode, the first to proclaim that the old struggle between the steppe and sown land had been bypassed: the drama of history was now going to lie in the tension between the oceans and the land. The globe was circumnavigated for the first time; European ships bearing explorers, traders, pirates, or men who were something of all three penetrated every sea and harbour; and although the ancient civilizations of Islam, India, China, and Japan saw no need to alter their customs to take account of European innovations, the signal had been given for their fall. Portuguese and Spanish explorations gave far-flung overseas empires to both countries—and as many difficulties as benefits. Other countries—France, England, the Netherlands, Sweden, and Denmark—thought it both undesirable and unsafe not to seek such empire themselves; the Iberian monarchies were thus involved in a perpetual struggle to defend their acquisitions. Those battles entailed incessant expenditure, which was more, in the end, than the kingdoms' revenues could match. Financial weakness was one of the chief causes of the decline of Spain.

But by then the inadequacies of the monarchical system had been cruelly exposed in such episodes as the revolt of the Netherlands against its Spanish overlord, the defeat of Spain's Invincible Armada by England, and, worst of all, the snail's-pace development of the Spanish colonies in the New World. The Spanish king Charles V and his son Philip II were as able as all but a few monarchs in recorded history, but they could not overcome the structural weaknesses of hereditary monarchy. There was no mechanism by which they could devolve their most crushing duties onto their ministers, so government moved slowly, if at all. As lawful sovereigns they were bound by the customs of their numerous realms, which frequently blocked necessary measures but could not safely be challenged, as Philip found when he tried to rule the Netherlands autocratically. They also were unable to guarantee that their heirs would be their equals in ability. The only remedy discoverable within the system was for the king in effect to abdicate in favour of a chief minister. Unfortunately, a man equal to the task was seldom found, and no minister, however gifted, was ever safe from the constant intrigues and conspiracies of disgruntled courtiers. Problems tended to accumulate until they became unmanageable. The same difficulties eventually ruined the French monarchy as well.

REPRESENTATION AND CONSTITUTIONAL MONARCHY

Meanwhile, the republican tradition had never quite died out. The Dutch had emerged from their long struggle against Spain clinging triumphantly to their new religion and their ancient constitution, a somewhat ramshackle federation known as the United Provinces. Switzerland was another medieval confederation; Venice and Genoa were rigidly oligarchical republics.

In England, the rise of Parliament introduced a republican, if not a democratic, element into the workings of one of Europe's oldest kingdoms. The tradition of representative estates was first exploited by the Renaissance monarchy of Henry VIII and his children, the Tudors, and then unsuccessfully challenged by their successors, the Stuarts. The English Civil Wars (1642–51) remade all institutions and culminated in the execution of King Charles I; in the long period of aftershocks opponents of King James II called in a new king and queen, William III and Mary II. William was a Dutchman who was quite content to let Parliament take an unprecedentedly large share in government so long as it voted money for war against Louis XIV of France. He conceded, in short, full power of the purse to the House of Commons, and before long it became a maxim of the dominant Whig party that no man could be legally taxed without his own consent or that of his representatives. A radically new age had dawned.

The Whig system was called constitutional monarchy. The increasingly rationalist temper of the times, exemplified in the works of John Locke (1632–1704), finally buried some of the more blatantly mythological theories of government, such as the divine right of kings, and Parliament finally settled the issues that had so vexed the country by passing a series of measures that gave England a written fundamental law for the first time. Henceforth the country was to be ruled by a partnership between king and Parliament (in practice, between the king and the oligarchy of country gentlemen who controlled most parliamentary elections); and if many Englishmen looked with distaste on the squabbles of party politics, which were the sordid result of that arrangement, few could propose a plausible alternative. Tories drank toasts in private to the Stuart kings in exile across the water; republicans published eloquent pamphlets; and Sir Robert Walpole ruled for 21 years (1721–42) as the first prime minister of Great Britain (as the country was called after the merger of England and Scotland in 1707).

The secret of Walpole's strength lay in his ability to simultaneously please the king, give the country sound government finances, and command a majority in both houses of Parliament. He performed the last trick partly

Sir Robert Walpole, the first prime minister of Great Britain. Hulton Archive/Getty Images

by giving out sinecures, salaries, and titles to his supporters, partly by his superiority in debate, and partly by exploiting Whig fears of Tories and Roman Catholics. Those three elements—party interest, practical decision making, and party ideology—have in one form or another come to dominate most modern political systems where brute force is checked by law.

Even after Walpole's fall his arrangements continued. They were vindicated by the Seven Years' War (1756–63), when Britain defeated both the French and Spanish empires and emerged predominant in every ocean and (especially) in North America. Immediately afterward, modern republican ideology found its classical expression.

WHIGS AND TORIES

The Whigs and the Tories were two opposing political parties or factions in England, particularly during the 18th century. Originally "Whig" and "Tory" were terms of abuse introduced in 1679 during the heated struggle over the bill to exclude James, duke of York (afterward James II), from the succession. Whig—whatever its origin in Scottish Gaelic—was a term applied to horse thieves and, later, to Scottish Presbyterians; it connoted nonconformity and rebellion and was applied to those who claimed the power of excluding the heir from the throne. Tory was an Irish term suggesting a papist outlaw and was applied to those who supported the hereditary right of James despite his Roman Catholic faith.

The Glorious Revolution (1688–89) greatly modified the division in principle between the two parties, for it had been a joint achievement. Thereafter most Tories accepted something of the Whig doctrines of limited constitutional monarchy rather than divine-right absolutism. Under Queen Anne, the Tories represented the resistance, mainly by the country gentry, to religious toleration and foreign entanglements. Toryism became identified with Anglicanism and the squirearchy and Whiggism with the aristocratic, landowning families and the financial interests of the wealthy middle classes.

The death of Anne in 1714, the manner in which George I came to the throne as a nominee of the Whigs, and the flight (1715) of the Tory leader Henry St. John, 1st Viscount Bolingbroke, to France, conspired to destroy the political power of the Tories as a party. For nearly 50 years thereafter, rule was by aristocratic groups and connections, regarding themselves as Whigs by sentiment and tradition.

The reign of George III (1760–1820) brought a shift of meanings to the two words. No Whig Party as such existed at the time, only a series of aristocratic groups and family connections operating in Parliament through patronage and influence. Nor was there a Tory Party, only Tory sentiment, tradition, and temperament surviving among certain families and social groups.

After 1784 William Pitt the Younger emerged as the leader of a new Tory Party, which broadly represented the interests of the country gentry, the merchant classes, and official administerial groups. In opposition, a revived Whig Party, led by Charles James Fox, came to represent the interests of religious dissenters, industrialists, and others who sought electoral, parliamentary, and philanthropic reforms.

The French Revolution and the wars against France soon further complicated the division between parties. A large section of the more moderate Whigs deserted Fox and supported Pitt. After 1815 and a period of party confusion, there eventually emerged the conservatism of Sir Robert Peel and Benjamin Disraeli, earl of Beaconsfield, and the liberalism of Lord John Russell and William Ewart Gladstone, with the party labels of Conservative and Liberal assumed by each faction, respectively. Although the label Tory has continued to be used to designate the Conservative Party, Whig has ceased to have much political meaning.

THE AMERICAN AND FRENCH REVOLUTIONS

The limited British monarchy found it little easier to govern a seaborne empire than did the kings of France and Spain. If Britain's North American colonies were to grow in population and riches—so as to become sources of strength to the empire, not military and financial liabilities—they had to be given a substantial measure of religious, economic, and political autonomy. However, that gift could not be revoked. Once British policy had created a chain of more or less self-governing communities along the Atlantic seaboard—communities much like the city-states of old—it could not undo its own work, even when it found its clients unreasonable, small-minded, and recalcitrant. Thus, when the British government attempted to impose tighter rule from London, the old empire broke down in bickering about taxation and in rioting, rebellion, and civil war—in short, the American Revolution. From 1775 to 1783 the Anglo-Americans fought with determination and good luck against their former overlord, King George III, and in 1776 their leaders determined to be rid of him and the British Parliament forever. The principles on which they meant to found a new commonwealth were expounded in their Declaration of Independence:

> *We hold these truths to be self-evident, that all men are created equal, that they are endowed by their Creator with certain inalienable Rights, that among these are Life, Liberty and the pursuit of Happiness. That, to secure these rights, Governments are instituted among Men, deriving their just powers from the consent of the governed....*

The application of those principles was more difficult than their enunciation, and it took the Americans more

A Parisian mob storming the Bastille. The capture of the former fort turned government prison on July 14, 1789, marked the beginning of the French Revolution. MPI/Archive Photos/Getty Images

than a decade to create a suitable framework of government. When they did adopt a new constitution, it served them so well that it is still in operation. That durability is not unconnected with the fact that the Constitution of the United States of America opened the door to modern liberal democracy—democracy in which the liberty of the individual is paramount. "The consent of the governed" was agreed to be the key to governmental legitimacy, and in practice the phrase rapidly came to mean "the consent of the majority." The principle of representation was embodied in the U.S. Constitution (the first section of which was entirely devoted to the establishment of Congress, the American parliament); this implied that there was no necessary limit to the size of a successful republic. From

Plato to Jean-Jacques Rousseau, theorists had agreed that democracies had to be small, because by definition all their citizens had to be able to give their consent in person. Now that notion had been discarded.

The American example might have had little effect on Europe but for the French Revolution of 1789. The French had helped the Americans defeat the British, but the effort had been too much in the end for the monarchy's finances. To avert state bankruptcy the Estates-General were summoned for the first time in 175 years, and soon the whole government had been turned upside down. The French repudiated the divine right of kings, the ascendancy of the nobility, the privileges of the Roman Catholic Church, and the regional structure of old France. Finally, they set up a republic and cut off the king's head.

Unfortunately for peace, in destroying the monarchy the French Revolution also crowned its centuries-old labours. The kings had created the French state; the revolution made it stronger than ever. The kings had united their subjects in the quest for glory; now the nation made the quest its own. In the name of rationality, liberty, and equality (fraternity was not a foremost concern), France again went to war. The revolution had brought the idea of the nation-state to maturity, and soon it proved capable of conquering the Continent, for everywhere French armies went, the revolutionary creed went, too.

In all this the French Revolution was giving expression to a general longing for government to be devoted to the greatest happiness of the greatest number. But there was also considerable resistance, which increased as time went on, to receiving the benefits of modern government at the hands of the French. So the wars of Napoleon, which opened the 19th century with the victories of Marengo, Austerlitz, and Jena, ended in the defeat of Waterloo.

After further revolutions and wars, the century ended with the French Third Republic nervously on the defensive, for the facts of demography had tilted against France as population growth in Britain and Germany accelerated and French growth slowed down. Moreover, French society was still bitterly at odds with itself.

Yet, on the whole, the work of the French Revolution survived. However many changes of regime France endured (seven between 1814 and 1870), its institutions had been thoroughly democratized, and the underlying drift of events steadily reinforced that achievement. By mid-century universal manhood suffrage had been introduced, putting France in that respect on the same footing as the United States.

Britain, pursuing its own historical logic, evolved in much the same way; its oligarchs slowly and ungraciously consented to share political power with other classes rather than lose it altogether. By the end of the 19th century manhood suffrage was clearly at hand in Britain, too, and women would not be denied the vote for much longer. Smaller European countries took the same course, and so did the "white" dominions of the British Empire.

Everywhere, the representative principle combined with the necessities of government to produce the modern political party. Elections could be won only by organized factions; politicians could attain or retain power only by winning elections, and they could wield it only with the support of parliamentary majorities. Permanent parties resulted. The Industrial Revolution and continuing population growth made an elaborate state apparatus increasingly necessary; the word *bureaucracy* came into general use. The spread of education and prosperity made more citizens feel fully able to take part in politics, whether as voters or as statesmen. Modern government in the West thus defined itself as a blend of administration, party politics, and passionate individualism, the whole held together, deep into the 20th century, by the cement of an equally passionate nationalism.

NATIONALISM AND IMPERIALISM

The kingdom of Prussia and the empires of Austria and Russia readily learned from the French Revolution that it was necessary to rationalize government. They had been struggling along that path even before 1789. Carrying out the necessary changes proved exceedingly difficult. (Russia, with its sacred, autocratic monarchy, in some ways more like ancient Egypt than a modern country, made far too few changes until far too late.) Meanwhile, the libertarian and egalitarian components of the revolutionary legacy were rigidly resisted. The great dynasts, and the military aristocracies that supported them, had no intention of admitting their obsolescence. Although they were forced to make limited concessions between 1789 and World War I, the autocratic citadel of their power was never surrendered. Instead, the myth of the nation was adopted to reinforce the authority of the state.

Nationalism intensified the competitiveness that had always been a part of the European state system. Peoples, it emerged, could be as touchy about their prestige as monarchs. But for one hundred years there was no general war in Europe, leaving the powers free to pursue interests in other parts of the world. Asia and Africa thus came to feel the full impact of European expansion, as the Americas had felt it before. Only the Japanese proved to have the skill to adapt successfully to the new ways—taking what suited them and rejecting the rest. They kept their millennial sacred monarchy but modernized the armed forces. In 1895 they fought and won a war against China, which was sliding into chaos, and in 1905 they defeated a great power, Russia. However, Japan was wholly exceptional. Elsewhere, European power was irresistible. Britain gave up the attempt to govern overseas settlements of its own people directly—the experiment had proved fatal in America and nearly so in Canada—but it had no scruple about wielding direct rule over non-British peoples, above all in India. France, Germany, and the United States eagerly followed this example. The Netherlands, Spain, and Portugal clung to what they had, though the last two suffered great imperial losses as Mexico, Brazil, and other Latin American colonies shook off imperial rule. It seemed that before long the whole world would be ruled by half a dozen powers.

It did not turn out so, or not for long. The problem of governmental legitimacy in central, eastern, and southern Europe was too explosive. The obstinate conservatism of the dynasts proved fatal to more than monarchy. There were too many who regarded the dynastic states as unacceptable, either because they were the instruments of class oppression, or because they embodied foreign rule, or both. And the romantic tradition of the French Revolution—the fall of the Bastille, the Reign of Terror, the Jacobin dictatorship—helped to drive many of those critics into violent rebellion, permanent conspiracy, and corrosive cynicism about the claims of authority. Authority itself, corrupted by power and at the same time gnawingly aware of its own fragility, gambled on militarist adventures. The upshot was World War I and the revolutions that resulted from it, especially those in Russia in March and November 1917, which overthrew the tsardom and set up a new model of government.

CHAPTER 3

Government in the 20th and 21st Centuries

In cold fact, the new government that came to power in the Russian Revolution of 1917 (comprising the revolutions of March and November of that year) was not quite as new as many of its admirers and enemies believed. Tyranny—the oppressive government of brute force—was as old as civilization itself. The first dictator in something like the modern sense—an absolute ruler owing little or nothing to tradition and in theory untrammeled by any institution or social group—was Julius Caesar, the great-uncle of the emperor Augustus. Caesar took the title of dictator from that of an emergency Roman office, and his assassination in 44 BCE foreshadowed the fate of many of his later imitators. Napoleon was the first modern dictator, and he was copied in Latin America, where many a general seized power after the disintegration of the Spanish empire. During the mid-19th-century wars of Italian unification, Giuseppe Garibaldi, idolized as a heroic leader, was briefly recognized as the dictator of Sicily. Born in chaos, commonly sustained by violence, 20th-century dictatorship, as a mode of government, was always fundamentally unstable, however long it lasted; it was a distilled expression of that craving for order and hatred of perceived threats to order that had always been the justification for autocracy and monarchy. It enacted the belief that society was best governed by the discipline thought necessary in an army at war. Such, too, was the underlying principle of the Soviet Union, though it professed to be a democracy and to be guided by the most advanced and scientific social philosophy of its age.

COMMUNISM AND FASCISM

Vladimir Ilich Lenin and his followers, the Bolsheviks (later known as the Communist Party of the Soviet Union), won power in the turmoil of revolutionary Russia because they were abler and more unscrupulous than any other group. They retained and increased their power by force, but they argued that the theories of Karl Marx (1818–83), as developed by Lenin, were of universal, permanent, and all-sufficient validity, that the leadership of the Communist Party had a unique understanding of those theories and of the proper tactics for realizing them, and that therefore the party's will could never legitimately be resisted. All institutions of the Soviet state were designed primarily to assure the untrammeled power of the party, and no methods were spurned—from mass starvation to the murder of artists—in furtherance of that aim. Even the economic and military achievements of the regime were secondary to that overall purpose; its most characteristic institutions, after the party, were the secret police and the forced labour camps.

LENINISM

Leninism is the set of principles expounded by Vladimir I. Lenin, who was the preeminent figure in the Russian Revolution of 1917.

In the *Communist Manifesto* (1848), Karl Marx and Friedrich Engels defined communists as "the most advanced and resolute section of the working-class parties of every country, that section which pushes forward all others." This conception was fundamental to Leninist thought. Lenin saw the Communist Party as a highly committed intellectual elite who (1) had a scientific understanding of history and society in the light of Marxist principles, (2) were committed to ending capitalism and instituting socialism in its place, (3) were bent on forcing through this transition after having achieved political power, and (4) were committed to attaining this power by any means possible, including violence and revolution if necessary. Lenin's emphasis upon action by a small, deeply committed group stemmed both from the need for efficiency and discretion in the revolutionary movement and from an authoritarian bent that was present in all of his political thought. The authoritarian aspect of Leninism appeared also in its insistence upon the need for a "proletarian dictatorship" following the seizure of power, a dictatorship that in practice was exercised not by the workers but by the leaders of the Communist Party.

Lenin was not at all convinced that the workers would inevitably acquire the proper revolutionary and class consciousness of the communist elite; he was instead afraid that they would be content with the gains in living and working conditions obtained through trade-union activity. In this, Leninism differed from traditional Marxism, which predicted that material conditions would suffice to make workers conscious of the need for revolution. For Lenin, then, the communist elite—the "workers' vanguard"—was more than a catalytic agent that precipitated events along their inevitable course; it was an indispensable element.

In practice, Leninism's unrestrained pursuit of the socialist society resulted in the creation of a totalitarian state in the Soviet Union. Every aspect of the Soviet Union's political, economic, cultural, and intellectual life came to be regulated by the Communist Party in a strict and regimented fashion that would tolerate no opposition. The building of the socialist society proceeded under a new autocracy of Communist Party officials and bureaucrats. Marxism and Leninism originally expected that, with the triumph of the proletariat, the state that Marx had defined as the organ of class rule would "wither away" because class conflicts would come to an end. Communist rule in the Soviet Union resulted instead in the vastly increased power of the state apparatus. Terror was applied without hesitation, humanitarian considerations and individual rights were disregarded, and the assumption of the class character of all intellectual and moral life led to a relativization of the standards of truth, ethics, and justice. Leninism thus created the first modern totalitarian state.

The Soviet model found many imitators. Lenin's strictly disciplined revolutionary party, the only morality of which was unswerving obedience to the leader, was a particularly attractive example to those intent on seizing power in a world made chaotic by World War I. Benito Mussolini of Italy, who won power in 1922, modeled his National Fascist Party on the Leninists, but he also exploited Italian traditions (including that of Garibaldi) in his portrayal of himself as a heroic leader. The ideology he manufactured to justify his regime, fascism, combined strident nationalism with unrelenting bellicosity. Adolf Hitler of Germany added a vicious anti-Semitism

Joseph Stalin. Photos.com/Jupiterimages

and a lust for mass murder to that brew. Mao Zedong in China combined Leninism with a hatred of all the foreign imperialists who had reduced China to nullity. In the Soviet Union itself Lenin's successor and disciple, Joseph Stalin, outdid his master in building up his power by mass terror and party discipline. Fascist practices were to some extent adopted by the government of Japan, the Nationalist victors in the Spanish Civil War (1936–39), and others.

All in all, the post–World War I period was characterized by state criminality on an unprecedented scale. It unsurprisingly culminated in World War II, which was marked by even greater atrocities, of which Hitler's murder of six million Jews and millions of others in the Holocaust was the worst.

None of those tyrants can be said to have vindicated in practice their ostensible theories of government; fascism, in particular, was never more than an ideological sham, a facade behind which individuals competed shamelessly for power and wealth. Its only answer to the problems of peace was war. Terror and technology were all that kept their regimes afloat, yet in their time they undeniably had a certain prestige. Liberal democracy and liberal economics had apparently failed, suggesting to some minds that the future of government lay with totalitarianism. (George Orwell's novel *Nineteen Eighty-four* [1949] depicts the dangers of that possibility.) Indeed, after his country's victory in World War II Stalin was able to extend the Soviet model to 11 states in eastern and central Europe.

However, after Stalin's death in 1953, the Soviet empire began to lurch from crisis to crisis, never resolving its basic dilemma; party dictatorship condemned the Soviet Union and its vassal states to permanent inefficiency and unrest, while reform would destroy the communist ascendancy. In 1985 a new generation came to power under Mikhail

Gorbachev, who was willing to take enormous risks in order to revitalize the Soviet empire. Before long, though, the communist regimes in Europe disintegrated, and in 1991 the Soviet Union itself dissolved. It suddenly became clear to most of the world that the Leninist experiment had failed as definitively as that of the fascists a generation earlier.

LIBERAL DEMOCRACY

Meanwhile, liberal democracy had gotten its second wind. Although the democracies had failed to avert the world wars and the Great Depression, they crushed the Axis powers in World War II and warded off the rivalry of communism in the Cold War that followed. Those achievements were undoubtedly in large part attributable to the colossal strength of the United States, but that strength itself was largely created by the American system of government, especially in the hands of President Franklin D. Roosevelt. American success scarcely faltered when Roosevelt suddenly died in 1945: by the end of the 20th century the country was generally looked on as the world's only superpower. Yet the parallel success of many other democracies — and the fact that the American model could not really be exported, being closely adapted to specific American conditions — showed that there was more to the triumph of the West than Americanism.

The democratic system everywhere brought with it growing prosperity, the emancipation of women, recognition of the equal rights of law-abiding individuals and social groups (whatever their origins or beliefs), and a professed commitment to international cooperation. The turbulent processes of open debate and decision produced an economic order that was vastly more productive than communist command economies. This gave hope to Western

In February 1945 the Big Three leaders (left to right), Prime Minister of Britain Winston Churchill, President Franklin D. Roosevelt, and Premier Joseph Stalin of the Soviet Union, met for top-level policy discussions on the last stages of World War II and the structure of the postwar world. The conference took place at Yalta in the Crimea. U.S. Army Photo

democracies that the world's largest democracy, India, would before long not only overcome its many intractable problems but also economically catch up with China.

However, the prosperity of Western democracies, as well as their free markets and free political institutions, was putting enormous strain on the rest of the world, since the West used up far more of the globe's natural and human resources than the size of its population seemed to justify. Non-Western societies were also having to cope with the disproportionate effects of such problems as a rapidly growing population, global economic downturns, the HIV/AIDS pandemic, and the worldwide environmental issues of ozone depletion and global warming. It was natural for some countries threatened by the hurricane of change to cling, however futilely, to the shreds of tradition, or even to try to rebuild an order that had failed. So it was in parts of the Islamic world, where a resurgence of religious fundamentalism led to campaigns for the establishment of Islamic republics, following the example of Iran and the short-lived Taliban regime of Afghanistan. In other Islamic countries, however, these changes, especially the economic ones, eventually led to strong popular movements for democratic reform.

CHAPTER 4

Nondemocratic Forms of Government

Nondemocratic forms of government encompass a variety of political systems. Chief among them are nonconstitutional monarchy; aristocracy and its debased form, oligarchy; dictatorship, including military and other authoritarian forms; and totalitarianism, which is usually regarded as distinct from dictatorship, though the leaders of totalitarian states are naturally dictators.

MONARCHY

Monarchy is a political system based upon the undivided sovereignty or rule of a single person. The term applies to states in which supreme authority is vested in the monarch, an individual ruler who functions as the head of state and who achieves his position through heredity. Succession usually passes from father or mother to son or daughter or follows other arrangements within the family or the monarchical dynasty.

FUNCTIONS OF MONARCHIES

A monarchy consists of distinct but interdependent institutions—a government and a state administration on the one hand, and a court and a variety of ceremonies on the other—that provide for the social life of the members of the dynasty, their friends, and the associated elite. Monarchy thus entails not only a political-administrative organization but also a "court society," a term coined by

44

the 20th-century German-born sociologist Norbert Elias to designate various groups of nobility that are linked to the monarchical dynasty (or "royal" house) through a web of personal bonds. All such bonds are evident in symbolic and ceremonial proprieties.

During a given society's history there are certain changes and processes that create conditions conducive to the rise of monarchy. Because warfare was the main means of acquiring fertile land and trade routes, some of the most prominent monarchs in the ancient world made their initial mark as warrior-leaders. Thus, the military accomplishments of Octavian (later Augustus) led to his position as emperor and to the institution of monarchy in the Roman Empire. Infrastructural programs and state-building also contributed to the development of monarchies. The need, common in arid cultures, to allocate fertile land and manage a regime of fresh water distribution (what the German-American historian Karl Wittfogel called hydraulic civilization) accounted for the founding of the ancient Chinese, Egyptian, and Babylonian monarchies on the banks of rivers. The monarchs also had to prove themselves as state-builders.

Monarchy also results from the wish of a society—be it a city population, tribe, or multi-tribal "people"—to groom an indigenous leader who will properly represent its historical goals and advance its interests. Monarchy, therefore, rests on the cultural identity and symbolism of the society it represents, and in so doing it reifies that identity within the society while also projecting it to outsiders. Perhaps most importantly, successful and popular monarchs were believed to have a sacred right to rule: some were regarded as gods (as in the case of the Egyptian pharaohs or the Japanese monarchs), some were crowned by priests, others were designated by prophets (King David of Israel), and still others were theocrats, leading both the religious and political spheres of their society—as did the caliphs of the Islamic state from the 7th century CE. Coming from these varying backgrounds, leaders first rose to power on the grounds of their abilities and charisma. Accordingly, monarchies proved capable of adapting to various social structures while also enduring dynamic cultural and geopolitical conditions. Thus, some ancient monarchies evolved as small city-states while others became large empires, the Roman Empire being the most conspicuous example.

PREMODERN MONARCHIES

During the Middle Ages, European monarchies underwent a process of evolution and transformation. Traditions of theocratic kingship, which were based on Roman and Christian precedents, emerged in the early centuries of the period, leading kings to assume their status as God's representatives on earth. Early medieval monarchs functioned as rulers of their people (rather than as territorial lords), and each was responsible for their people's protection. In the 11th century, however, the Gregorian Reform, and the Investiture Controversy associated with it, undermined the claims of theocratic kingship, and monarchs—most notably the emperors—looked to Roman law for new justification of their right to rule. Throughout the Middle Ages, kings had come to power through conquest, acclamation, election, or inheritance. Medieval monarchs ruled through their courts, which were at first private households but from the 12th century developed into more formal and institutional bureaucratic structures. It was during the 12th century as well that kings evolved into rulers of people and of territories with defined borders. By the end of the Middle Ages, the development of the territorial monarchies had laid the foundation for the idea of the modern nation-state.

Painting of a Japanese warlord being named shogun. In the late 12th century Japanese monarchs ruled in name only; the real power lay within various shogunates. Time & Life Pictures/Getty Images

Unlike in Europe, the Islamic monarchy, the caliphate, remained unified and theocratic, combining religious and lay functions. In Japan, the monarchy conceded real power to the shogunate, which was technically controlled by the emperor but in practice dominated by the shogun, a supreme warlord. Attempts to attain this position often resulted in inter-dynastic conflict. In China, the monarchy evolved as a centralized bureaucratic body, held by a succession of various dynasties.

The Renaissance and early modern period led to a newly adapted type of monarchy in Europe, with monarchs initiating voyages of discovery to other continents, developing new forms of mercantile trade, and, most of all, building mass armies and large government bureaucracies that represented innovative forms of political administration. Compared to their predecessors, the monarchs of this era were better able to monitor and manage their own societies, to exact more taxes, and to decide on interstate war and conquest. The Renaissance monarchs, such as Charles V (reigned 1519–56), Francis I (1515–47), and Elizabeth I (1558–1603), unified their realms and strengthened their bureaucracies. However, later monarchs, such as Catherine the Great of Russia (reigned 1762–96), Louis XIV of France (1643–1715), and Frederick the Great of Prussia (1740–86), symbolized "absolutist" rule, as exemplified by Louis XIV's declaration, *"L'état, c'est moi"* ("I am the state"). Possessing complete administrative and military power, an absolute monarch could bypass the feudal lords or subjugate independent city-states and run his kingdom with individual autonomy or arbitrariness.

Yet in most cases absolute monarchy was absolutist only in appearance. In practice, most monarchs remained dependent upon chosen administrators to whom they had delegated the authority to govern their states, as was the case in France. These officials were checked by institutions such as England's Parliament, or balanced by factions of the landed aristocracy, as in Russia and Poland. Monarchs were thus able to exploit their power, adding onto their traditional legitimacies while allowing for certain checks on their regimes, all of which seemed to portend continuous stability, had changes in the prevailing social and economic order not challenged the future of absolutist monarchies. One force of change, the Reformation (and the factionalism associated with it), triggered protracted religious conflicts, while the Industrial Revolution unleashed social unrest and class conflict—all of which occurred amid ongoing developments in international trade, investments, and other complex financial transactions that provoked economic problems such as inflation.

Most importantly, new perceptions emerged, first in Europe and then in the Middle East, Asia, and Africa, that reduced the monarchs' authority. The concept of "divine right" was often eroded by the spread of secularism. Emerging ideas of the individual's natural rights (as espoused by the philosophers John Locke and Jean-Jacques Rousseau and further evidenced by the Declaration of Independence of the United States) and those of nations' rights (particularly regarding independence and self-determination) gained prominence. Moreover, the monarchs' traditional supremacy, anchored in their lineage as descendants of war heroes and of leading notables, gradually weakened in favour of what the German-born American sociologist Reinhard Bendix called "a mandate of the people." Thus, a society's "sovereignty," or its principles of independence, cohesion, and leadership, rested with its people as a whole and not with an individual and his dynasty.

Monarchies were therefore challenged by various opposition movements. Although the British monarchy was able to cope with religious strife as well as social unrest among the rural and urban lower classes, the monarchies in France (beginning in 1789), Russia (1917), and China (1911) were swept away by popular social revolutions. The Austrian, German, and Ottoman monarchies also collapsed after World War I, having been defeated militarily and replaced by indigenous nationalist movements. It then became evident that monarchies could survive only if they were built upon a foundation of broad, nationalist-popular support, benefiting from a majority coalition of social forces.

MONARCHY IN THE MODERN ERA

When he crowned himself Emperor of France in 1804 (and ratified the act by a people's referendum), Napoleon

Bonaparte instituted a new type of monarchy. This was the "nationalist monarchy," whereby the monarch ruled on behalf of his society's nationalist aspirations and drive for independence (as opposed to the earlier types of legitimacy). Napoleon based his rule on the instruments of the French Revolution, such as the Declaration of the Rights of Man and of the Citizen. He was also, however, an absolutist monarch who installed his family members as rulers in several European states that had fallen under his control.

DECLARATION OF THE RIGHTS OF MAN AND OF THE CITIZEN

The Declaration of the Rights of Man and of the Citizen, known in French as the *Declaration des Droits de l'Homme et du Citoyen*, was one of the basic charters of human liberties, containing the principles that inspired the French Revolution. Its 17 articles, adopted between August 20 and August 26, 1789, by France's National Assembly, served as the preamble to the Constitution of 1791. Similar documents served as the preamble to the Constitution of 1793 (retitled simply Declaration of the Rights of Man) and to the Constitution of 1795 (retitled Declaration of the Rights and Duties of Man and the Citizen).

The basic principle of the Declaration was that all "men are born and remain free and equal in rights" (Article 1), which were specified as the rights of liberty, private property, the inviolability of the person, and resistance to oppression (Article 2). All citizens were equal before the law and were to have the right to participate in legislation directly or indirectly (Article 6); no one was to be arrested without a judicial order (Article 7). Freedom of religion (Article 10) and freedom of speech (Article 11) were safeguarded within the bounds of public "order" and "law." The document reflects the interests of the elites who wrote it: property was given the status of an inviolable right, which could be taken by the state only if an indemnity were given (Article 17); offices and position were opened to all citizens (Article 6).

The sources of the Declaration included the major thinkers of the French Enlightenment, such as Montesquieu, who had urged the separation of powers, and Jean-Jacques Rousseau, who wrote of general will—the concept that the state represents the general will of the citizens. The idea that the individual must be safeguarded against arbitrary police or judicial action was anticipated by the 18th-century *parlements*, as well as by writers such as Voltaire. French jurists and economists such as the physiocrats had insisted on the inviolability of private property. Other influences on the authors of the Declaration were foreign documents such as the Virginia Declaration of Rights (1776) in North America and the manifestos of the Dutch Patriot movement of the 1780s. The French Declaration went beyond these models, however, in its scope and in its claim to be based on principles that are fundamental to man and therefore universally applicable.

On the other hand, the Declaration is also explicable as an attack on the pre-Revolutionary monarchical regime. Equality before the law was to replace the system of privileges that characterized the old regime. Judicial procedures were insisted upon to prevent abuses by the king or his administration, such as the *lettre de cachet*, a private communication from the king, often used to give summary notice of imprisonment.

Having taken root in Europe, nationalist monarchies spread to other parts of the world. In the 19th and early 20th centuries, new monarchs came to power in Greece and the Arab provinces (notably Egypt and Syria) and in states that had gained independence from the Ottoman

Empire and the Austro-Hungarian Empire. The monarchs of this era wished to emphasize the modern identity of their nations, and in so doing they attempted to use their imperial titles as proof of modernity, even as they aspired to achieve equal footing with established, prominent monarchs such as the British royalty. Their ultimate political influence, however, was limited: under their leadership political institutions failed to root themselves in society, and economies remained relatively underdeveloped. Unable to meet the needs of mass societies, the nationalist monarchs could not withstand the waves of major opposition movements, typical of the mid-20th century, which were either anticolonial, nationalist, or Marxist. These movements regarded all monarchies as bastions of an old, obsolete order that had to be eradicated. Monarchs were blamed for social injustice, political corruption, and economic backwardness, and they were consequently overthrown. Monarchies had acquired an image of a defeated, outdated system.

This mainly typified the absolutist monarchies led by rulers who exercised full authority as heads of states. In the midst of this, however, emerged a group of European monarchies that adapted to the new challenges. These became the "constitutional monarchies," the leading contemporary examples of which are the United Kingdom, Belgium, the Netherlands, Norway, Sweden, and Denmark. In these states, a legacy of political bargaining has existed, witnessing the monarch's gradual transfer of authority to various societal groups. Although the monarch remains the head of state and the emblem of state authority, the sovereign accepts that this authority has been transposed to that of a formal position, and the monarch waives actual political power, which is assumed by the people. In such monarchies political authority is exercised by elected politicians, and the political process runs according to democratic procedures. Hence, the monarch functions as a unifying and symbolic head of state who performs ceremonial duties, while the monarchical traditions and ceremonies have become national assets that symbolize historical continuity.

By the early 21st century, examples of traditional monarchies were largely limited to the Arab world. These included the six oil-rich states, located along the Persian Gulf—Kuwait, Saudi Arabia, Bahrain, Qatar, the United Arab Emirates, and Oman—as well as Jordan and Morocco. In the second decade of the century, however, some of these regimes were threatened by a wave of popular democratic revolts that swept through large parts of the Middle East. Their longevity until that time could only partially be accounted for by the abundance of oil revenues that made it possible for their monarchs to overpower any opposition groups. Jordan and Morocco, after all, were not awash in oil wealth but were among the most stable regimes in the region. The fact that many of these states benefited from U.S. and British military support certainly accounted for some of their perseverance in the face of external threats.

The historical stability of Arab monarchies rested largely upon their political and cultural underpinnings, where the idea of a single hereditary ruler—or, rather, a single hereditary ruling family—maintained a high degree of social currency. In the case of the Persian Gulf states, local monarchies thrived by grafting themselves to the existing tribal framework. Such a system differs significantly from the concept of monarchy found in other parts of the world inasmuch as power lies in the hands of a ruling family—an extended entity whose members can number in the thousands—rather than in the hands of a single individual. In that system, the king is merely the head of the ruling family, a situation that early European scholars of the Middle

East described by recycling the phrase *primus inter pares* ("first among equals"). Just as the monarch is the *primus inter pares* in the ruling family, the ruling family itself is the *primus inter pares* among the tribes of a given country. In such a situation, the ruling family maintains its position by mollifying dissenting opinions, addressing grievances, distributing largesse, and, when necessary, squelching extreme views through the selective use of coercive power. (In Saudi Arabia, the monarchy also relied to a great extent on religious legitimacy.) Such political systems can be loosely described as pluralistic, since membership in any extended family group or tribe grants one a voice in ongoing events. Those outside the tribal system, however, often have little political voice. The monarch and his family maintain political stability by managing events and by building political alliances. Stability was further advanced in the Persian Gulf monarchies by the fact that a significant portion of the population belongs to the royal family. Under rare circumstances, the royal family will dethrone a monarch if his inattention or incompetence threaten the family's place at the head of society. Such an event occurred when Saʻūd, king of Saudi Arabia, was dethroned in 1964.

The monarchies of Morocco and Jordan, both of which resembled traditional monarchies, thrived for different reasons. In Morocco, the king was also a religious figure of great importance. In Jordan, the Hashemite monarchy owed its longevity to the exceptional political acumen of Hussein ibn Ṭalāl (reigned 1953–99), which secured political power for the family.

The ruling families of the gulf Arab states proved themselves effective state-builders by introducing technological innovations and social modernity into their societies while enforcing a conservative political atmosphere. Such monarchies proved to be effective integrators of their societies. They did not achieve this by enforcing a new, socialist, Arab-nationalist, and revolutionary character on society—as did revolutionary states such as Syria and Egypt in the mid-20th century. Instead they waived that pretension to create a uniform society and permitted socio-cultural variety, intended to befit traditional sentiments.

ARISTOCRACY, OLIGARCHY, AND DICTATORSHIP

While royal rule, as legitimized by blood descent, has mostly vanished as an effective principle of government in the modern world, other nondemocratic forms of government, including aristocracy, oligarchy, and dictatorship, continue to exist. The last form was prevalent at one time or another in most regions of the world outside North America until the late 20th century. Indeed, the 20th century—which encompassed the careers of Benito Mussolini, Adolf Hitler, Joseph Stalin, Francisco Franco, Mao Zedong, Juan Perón, Sukarno, François ("Papa Doc") Duvalier, Ferdinand Marcos, and Augusto Pinochet—might fairly be described by future historians as the age of dictatorship.

ARISTOCRACY

Aristocracy is a form of government in which power is wielded by a relatively small privileged class or by a minority consisting of those considered to be best qualified to rule.

As conceived by the Greek philosophers Plato (*c.* 428–*c.* 348 BCE) and Aristotle (384–322 BCE), aristocracy means the rule of the few best—the morally and intellectually superior—governing in the interest of the entire population. Such a form of government differs from the rule of one (by a monarchy or by a tyrant, or dictator), of the ambitious, self-interested, or greedy few (oligarchy or timocracy), or of the many (democracy or mobocracy).

An Indonesian Brahman priest, photographed in the 1950s. The Brahman constitute the highest-ranking Hindu social caste in India. Richard Harrington/Hulton Archive/Getty Images

Because "the best" is an evaluative and subjective notion, it is difficult to distinguish aristocratic from oligarchic governments objectively. Moreover, because a monarchical system has its own aristocracy and because the people try to elect the best as their rulers in democracies, an aristocratic element also is present in these regimes. For these reasons, the term *aristocracy* often is used to mean the ruling upper layer of a stratified group. Thus, the upper ranks of the government form the political aristocracy of the state; the stratum of the highest religious dignitaries constitutes the aristocracy of the church; and the richest captains of industry and finance constitute an aristocracy of economic wealth.

The Brahman caste in India, the Spartiates in Sparta, the eupatridae in Athens, the patricians or Optimates in Rome, and the medieval nobility in Europe are various historical examples of the social aristocracy or nobility. Most such social aristocracies, both legally and factually, have been hereditary. Other aristocracies have been nonhereditary and recruited from different strata of the population, such as the upper stratum of the Roman Catholic Church, the ruling aristocracy of elective republics and monarchies, the leaders of scientific and artistic organizations, and certain aristocracies of wealth.

The distinction between aristocracy of birth and non-hereditary aristocracy is relative, because even in caste societies some low-born persons climb into the higher castes and some high-born persons slide into the lower castes. On the other hand, even in open aristocracies there is a tendency for the upper stratum to become a hereditary group filled mainly by the offspring of aristocratic parents. For example, among millionaires and billionaires living in the United States at the beginning of the 21st century, the percentage born of wealthy parents is notably higher than among American millionaires of the mid-19th century.

OLIGARCHY

Oligarchy is a form of aristocratic government in which the ruling group or class exercises power for its own corrupt or selfish purposes and not for the benefit of the state or the people.

Aristotle used the term *oligarchia* to designate the rule of the few when it was exercised not by the best but by bad men unjustly. In this sense, oligarchy is a debased form of aristocracy. Most classic oligarchies have resulted when governing elites were recruited exclusively from a ruling caste—a hereditary social grouping that is set apart from the rest of society by religion, kinship, economic status, prestige, or even language. Such elites tend to exercise power in the interests of their own class.

It is a recurrent idea that all forms of government are in the final analysis reducible to the rule of a few. Oligarchs will secure effective control whether the formal authority is vested in the people, a monarch, the proletariat, or a dictator. Thus, Karl Marx and Friedrich Engels insisted that, throughout capitalism, the key capitalists had controlled the government; they coined the dictum, "The state is the executive committee of the exploiting class." The Italian political scientist Gaetano Mosca likewise insisted that a "ruling class" always exercised effective oligarchic control. Vilfredo Pareto elaborated the idea in his doctrine of the "elite." The modern tendency to analyze social patterns in terms of an "elite," although greatly reinforced by Pareto's theory, goes further back than Marx and Engels, who employed the term *elite* to describe the class-conscious communists, the leading group within the proletariat.

One of the most famous modern uses of the term occurs in the phrase "iron law of oligarchy," which was coined by the German sociologist Robert Michels to refer to the alleged inevitable tendency of political parties and trade unions to become bureaucratized, centralized, and conservative. His reasoning was that, no matter how egalitarian or even radical the original ideology and goals of a party or union may be, there must emerge a limited group of leaders at the centre who can direct power efficiently, get things done through an administrative staff, and evolve some kind of rigorous order and ideology to ensure the survival of the organization when faced by internal division and external opposition. Subsequent writers of various persuasions have attempted either to expand on Michels's thesis, extending it to legislatures, religious orders, and other organizations, or to restrict or criticize the thesis, charging that the iron law of oligarchy is not universal and that some unions and parties do maintain a viable system of democratic expression and governance.

As discussed in the following section, beginning in the mid-20th century the governments of some newly independent countries, including former colonial states in Africa and Asia, gradually deteriorated into oligarchic and dictatorial forms. Oligarchy and dictatorship were also characteristic of many Latin American states until the late 20th century. Following the formal dissolution of the Soviet Union in 1991, the economy of the new Russian Federation came under the control of oligarchs, who by virtue of their great wealth exercised considerable political power.

DICTATORSHIP

Dictatorship is a form of government in which one person or a small group of people possesses absolute power without effective constitutional limitations. The term *dictatorship* comes from the Latin title dictator, which in the Roman Republic designated a temporary magistrate who was granted extraordinary powers in order to deal with state crises. Modern dictators, however, resemble ancient tyrants rather than ancient dictators. Ancient philosophers' descriptions of the tyrannies of Greece and Sicily go far toward characterizing modern dictatorships. Dictators usually resort to force or fraud to gain despotic political power, which they maintain through the use of intimidation, terror, and the suppression of basic civil liberties. They may also employ techniques of mass propaganda in order to sustain their public support.

With the decline and disappearance in the 19th and 20th centuries of monarchies based on hereditary descent, dictatorship became one of the two chief forms of government in use by nations throughout the world, the other being constitutional democracy. Rule by dictators has taken several different forms. In Latin America in the 19th century, various dictators arose after effective central authority had collapsed in the new nations recently freed from Spanish colonial rule. These *caudillos*, or self-proclaimed leaders, usually led a private army and tried to establish control over a territory before marching upon a weak national government. Antonio López de Santa Anna in Mexico and Juan Manuel de Rosas in Argentina are examples of such leaders. Later 20th-century dictators in Latin America were different. They were national rather than provincial leaders and often were put in their position of power by nationalistic military officers, as was Juan Perón of Argentina. They usually allied themselves with a particular social class, and attempted either to support an oligarchy of wealthy and privileged elites or to institute far-reaching left-wing social reforms.

In the new states of Africa and Asia after World War II, dictators quickly established themselves on the ruins of constitutional arrangements inherited from the Western colonial powers that had proved unworkable in the absence of a strong middle class and in the face of local traditions of autocratic rule. In some such countries,

Mustafa Kemal (Atatürk) in 1923. UPI/Bettmann Newsphotos

elected presidents and prime ministers captured personal power by establishing one-party rule and suppressing the opposition, while in others the army seized power and established military dictatorships.

Many scholars make a distinction between military or other authoritarian dictatorships and totalitarianism.

Authoritarian regimes (unlike totalitarian ones) usually have no highly developed guiding ideology, tolerate some pluralism in social organization, lack the power to mobilize the entire population in pursuit of national goals, and exercise the power they do have within relatively predictable limits. The pro-Western military dictatorships of Latin America, including Paraguay under Alfredo Stroessner and Chile under Augusto Pinochet, are examples of authoritarian regimes, according to this view. In contrast, in totalitarian dictatorships an official ideology is used to legitimize and maintain the regime, the state is identified with a single mass party and the party with its charismatic leader, extensive terror and propaganda are used to suppress dissent and stifle opposition, and science and technology are employed to control the economy and individual behaviour. The chief modern examples of totalitarianism are the fascist dictatorship of Adolf Hitler in Nazi Germany (1933–45) and the communist dictatorship of Joseph Stalin in the Soviet Union (1924–53). Soviet-type communist dictatorships also arose in central and eastern Europe, China, and other countries in the wake of World War II, though most of them (as well as the Soviet Union itself) had collapsed by the last decade of the 20th century.

During times of domestic or foreign crisis, even most constitutional governments have conferred emergency powers on the chief executive, and in some notable cases this provided the opportunity for duly elected leaders to overthrow democracy and rule dictatorially thereafter. The proclamation of emergency rule, for example, was the beginning of the dictatorships of Hitler in Germany, Benito Mussolini in Italy, Kemal Atatürk in Turkey, Józef Piłsudski in Poland, and António de Oliveira Salazar in Portugal. In other democracies, however, constitutional arrangements have survived quite lengthy periods of crisis, as in Great Britain and the United States during World War II, in which the use of extraordinary powers by the executive came to a halt with the end of the wartime emergency.

TOTALITARIANISM

Totalitarianism is a form of government that theoretically permits no individual freedom and that seeks to subordinate all aspects of the individual's life to the authority of the government. Italian dictator Benito Mussolini coined the term *totalitario* in the early 1920s to describe the new fascist state of Italy, which he further described as: "All within the state, none outside the state, none against the state." By the beginning of World War II, "totalitarian" had become synonymous with absolute and oppressive single-party government.

In the broadest sense, totalitarianism is characterized by strong central rule that attempts to control and direct all aspects of individual life through coercion and repression. Examples of such centralized totalitarian rule include the Maurya dynasty of India (*c.* 321–*c.* 185 BCE), the Ch'in dynasty of China (221–206 BCE), and the reign of Zulu chief Shaka (*c.* 1816–28). The totalitarian states of Nazi Germany under Adolf Hitler and the Soviet Union under Joseph Stalin were the first examples of decentralized or popular totalitarianism, in which the state achieved overwhelming popular support for its leadership. This support was not spontaneous; its genesis depended on a charismatic leader; and it was made possible only by modern developments in communication and transportation.

Totalitarianism is often distinguished from authoritarian dictatorship, despotism, or tyranny by its supplanting of all political institutions with new ones and its sweeping away of all legal, social, and political traditions. The totalitarian state pursues some special goal, such as industrialization or conquest, to the exclusion of all others. All resources are directed toward its attainment regardless of the cost. Whatever might further the goal is supported; whatever might foil the goal is rejected. This obsession spawns an ideology that explains everything in terms of the goal, rationalizing all obstacles that may arise and all forces that may contend with the state. The resulting popular support permits the state the widest latitude of action of any form of government. Any dissent is branded evil, and internal political differences are not permitted. Because pursuit of the goal is the only ideological foundation for the totalitarian state, achievement of the goal can never be acknowledged.

Under totalitarian rule, traditional social institutions and organizations are discouraged and suppressed; thus the social fabric is weakened and people become more amenable to absorption into a single, unified movement. Participation in approved public organizations is at first encouraged and then required. Old religious and social ties are supplanted by artificial ties to the state and its ideology. As pluralism and individualism diminish, most of the people embrace the totalitarian state's ideology. The infinite diversity among individuals blurs, replaced by a mass conformity (or at least acquiescence) to the beliefs and behaviour sanctioned by the state.

Large-scale, organized violence becomes permissible and sometimes necessary under totalitarian rule, justified by the overriding commitment to the state ideology and pursuit of the state's goal. In Nazi Germany and Stalin's Soviet Union, whole classes of people, such as the Jews and the kulaks (wealthy peasant farmers) respectively, were singled out for persecution and extinction. In each case the persecuted were linked with some external enemy and blamed for the state's troubles, and thereby public opinion was aroused against them and their fate at the hands of the military and the police was condoned.

Police operations within a totalitarian state often appear similar to those within a police state, but one important difference distinguishes them. In a police state the police operate according to known, consistent procedures. In a totalitarian state the police operate without the constraints of laws and regulations. Their actions are unpredictable and directed by the whim of their rulers. Under Hitler and Stalin uncertainty was interwoven into the affairs of the state. The German constitution of the Weimar Republic was never abrogated under Hitler, but an enabling act passed by the Reichstag in 1933 permitted him to amend the constitution at will, in effect nullifying it. The role of lawmaker became vested in one man. Similarly, Stalin provided a constitution for the Soviet Union in 1936 but never permitted it to become the framework of Soviet law. Instead, he was the final arbiter in the interpretation of Marxism–Leninism–Stalinism and changed his interpretations at will. Neither Hitler nor Stalin permitted change to become predictable, thus increasing the sense of terror among the people and repressing any dissent.

CHAPTER 5

Prehistoric Democracy to the Italian Republics

D emocracy is a political system in which the people rule themselves, either directly by vote or consensus on all matters of public concern or indirectly by means of the vote of representatives. The term is derived from the Greek *demokratia*, which was coined from *demos* ("people") and *kratos* ("rule") in the middle of the 5th century BCE to denote the political systems then existing in some Greek city-states, notably Athens.

FUNDAMENTAL PROBLEMS OF DEMOCRACY

The etymological origins of the term *democracy* hint at a number of urgent problems that go far beyond semantic issues. If a government of or by the people—a "popular" government—is to be established, at least five fundamental questions must be confronted at the outset, and two more are almost certain to be posed if the democracy continues to exist for long.

1. What is the appropriate unit or association within which a democratic government should be established? A town or city? A country? A business corporation? A university? An international organization? All of these?
2. Given an appropriate association—a city, for example—who among its members should enjoy full citizenship? Which persons, in other

66

words, should constitute the *dēmos?* Is every member of the association entitled to participate in governing it? Assuming that children should not be allowed to participate (as most adults would agree), should the demos include all adults? If it includes only a subset of the adult population, how small can the subset be before the association ceases to be a democracy and becomes something else, such as an aristocracy (government by the best, *aristos*) or an oligarchy (government by the few, *oligos*)?

3. Assuming a proper association and a proper *dēmos*, how are citizens to govern? What political organizations or institutions will they need? Will these institutions differ between different kinds of associations—for example, a small town and a large country?

4. When citizens are divided on an issue, as they often will be, whose views should prevail, and in what circumstances? Should a majority always prevail, or should minorities sometimes be empowered to block or overcome majority rule?

5. If a majority is ordinarily to prevail, what is to constitute a proper majority? A majority of all citizens? A majority of voters? Should a proper majority comprise not individual citizens but certain groups or associations of citizens, such as hereditary groups or territorial associations?

6. The preceding questions presuppose an adequate answer to a sixth and even more important question: Why should "the people" rule? Is democracy really better than aristocracy or monarchy? Perhaps, as Plato argues in the *Republic*, the best government would be led by a minority of the most highly

qualified persons—an aristocracy of "philosopher-kings." What reasons could be given to
show that Plato's view is wrong?

7. No association could maintain a democratic
government for very long if a majority of the
dēmos—or a majority of the government—
believed that some other form of government
were better. Thus, a minimum condition for
the continued existence of a democracy is that
a substantial proportion of both the *dēmos* and
the leadership believes that popular government is better than any feasible alternative.
What conditions, in addition to this one,
favour the continued existence of democracy?
What conditions are harmful to it? Why have
some democracies managed to endure, even
through periods of severe crisis, while so many
others have collapsed?

Since the time of the ancient Greeks, both the theory
and the practice of democracy have undergone profound
changes, many of which have concerned the prevailing
answers to questions (1) through (3) above. Thus, for thousands of years the kind of association in which democracy
was practiced, the tribe or the city-state, was small enough
to be suitable for some form of democracy by assembly,
or "direct democracy." Much later, beginning in the 18th
century, as the typical association became the nation-state
or country, direct democracy gave way to representative
democracy—a transformation so sweeping that, from
the perspective of a citizen of ancient Athens, the governments of gigantic associations such as France or the
United States might not have appeared democratic at all.
This change, in turn, entailed a new answer to question (3):
Representative democracy would require a set of political

institutions radically different from those of all earlier democracies.

Another important change has concerned the prevailing answers to question (2). Until fairly recently, most democratic associations limited the right to participate in government to a minority of the adult population—indeed, sometimes to a very small minority. Beginning in the 20th century, this right was extended to nearly all adults. Accordingly, a contemporary democrat could reasonably argue

A suffragette petitioning for the right to vote. In a democracy, the right to participate in governing through voting historically has gone from being the right of a few to the right of many. Library of Congress Prints and Photographs Division

that Athens, because it excluded so many adults from the *dēmos*, was not really a democracy—even though the term *democracy* was invented and first applied in Athens.

Despite these and other important changes, it is possible to identify a considerable number of early political systems that involved some form of "rule by the people," even if they were not fully democratic by contemporary standards.

PREHISTORIC FORMS OF DEMOCRACY

Although it is tempting to assume that democracy was created in one particular place and time—most often identified as Greece about the year 500 BCE—evidence suggests that democratic government, in a broad sense, existed in several areas of the world well before the turn of the 5th century.

It is plausible to assume that democracy in one form or another arises naturally in any well-bounded group, such as a tribe, if the group is sufficiently independent of control by outsiders to permit members to run their own affairs and if a substantial number of members, such as tribal elders, consider themselves about equally qualified to participate in decisions about matters of concern to the group as a whole. This assumption has been supported by studies of nonliterate tribal societies, which suggest that democratic government existed among many tribal groups during the thousands of years when human beings survived by hunting and gathering. To these early humans, democracy, such as it was practiced, might well have seemed the most "natural" political system.

When the lengthy period of hunting and gathering came to an end and humans began to settle in fixed communities, primarily for agriculture and trade, the conditions that favour popular participation in government seem to have become rare. Greater inequalities in wealth and military power between communities, together with a marked increase in the typical community's size and scale, encouraged the spread of hierarchical and authoritarian forms of social organization. As a result, popular governments among settled peoples vanished, to be replaced for thousands of years by governments based on monarchy, despotism, aristocracy, or oligarchy, each of which came to be seen—at least among the dominant members of these societies—as the most natural form of government.

Then, about 500 BCE, conditions favourable to democracy reappeared in several places, and a few small groups began to create popular governments. Primitive democracy, one might say, was reinvented in more advanced forms. The most crucial developments occurred in two areas of the Mediterranean, Greece and Rome.

CLASSICAL GREECE

During the Classical period (corresponding roughly to the 5th and 4th centuries BCE), Greece was of course not a country in the modern sense but a collection of several hundred independent city-states, each with its surrounding countryside. In 507 BCE, under the leadership of Cleisthenes, the citizens of Athens began to develop a system of popular rule that would last nearly two centuries. To question (1), then, the Greeks responded clearly: The political association most appropriate to democratic government is the polis, or city-state.

Athenian democracy foreshadowed some later democratic practices, even among peoples who knew little or nothing of the Athenian system. Thus the Athenian answer to question (2)—Who should constitute the *dēmos?*—was similar to the answer developed in many newly democratic countries in the 19th and 20th centuries. Although citizenship in Athens was hereditary, extending to anyone who was born to parents who were themselves Athenian citizens, membership in the *dēmos* was limited to male citizens 18 years of age or older (until 403, when the minimum age was raised to 20).

Because data is scanty, estimates of the size of the Athenian *dēmos* must be treated with caution. One scholar has suggested that in the mid-4th century there may have been about 100,000 citizens, 10,000 resident foreigners, or metics, and as many as 150,000 slaves. Among citizens, about 30,000 were males over 18. If these numbers are roughly correct, then the *dēmos* comprised 10 to 15 percent of the total population.

Regarding question (3)—What political institutions are necessary for governing?—the Athenians adopted an answer that would appear independently elsewhere. The heart and centre of their government was the Assembly (Ecclesia), which met almost weekly—40 times a year—on the Pnyx, a hill west of the Acropolis. Decisions were taken by vote, and, as in many later assemblies, voting was by a show of hands. As would also be true in many later democratic systems, the votes of a majority of those present and voting prevailed. Although we have no way of knowing how closely the majority in the Assembly represented the much larger number of eligible citizens who did not attend, given the frequency of meetings and the accessibility of the meeting place, it is unlikely that the Assembly could have long persisted in making markedly unpopular decisions.

The powers of the Assembly were broad, but they were by no means unlimited. The agenda of the Assembly was set by the Council of Five Hundred, which, unlike the Assembly, was composed of representatives chosen by lot from each of 139 small territorial entities, known as demes, created by Cleisthenes in 507. The number of representatives from each deme was roughly proportional to its population. The Council's use of representatives (though chosen by lot rather than by election) foreshadowed the election of representatives in later democratic systems.

Another important political institution in Athens was the popular courts (*dikasteria*), described by one scholar as "the most important organ of state, alongside the Assembly," with "unlimited power to control the Assembly, the Council, the magistrates, and political leaders." The popular courts were composed of jurors chosen by lot from a pool of citizens over 30 years of age; the pool itself was chosen annually and also by lot. The institution is a further illustration of the extent to which the ordinary citizens of Athens were expected to participate in the political life of the city.

In 411 BCE, exploiting the unrest created by Athens's disastrous and seemingly endless war with Sparta, a group known as the Four Hundred seized control of Athens and established an oligarchy. Less than a year later, the Four Hundred were overthrown and democracy was fully restored. Nine decades later, in 321, Athens was subjugated by its more powerful neighbour to the north, Macedonia, which introduced property qualifications that effectively excluded many ordinary Athenians from the *dēmos*. In 146 BCE what remained of Athenian democracy was extinguished by the conquering Romans.

THE ROMAN REPUBLIC

At about the same time that popular government was introduced in Greece, it also appeared on the Italian Peninsula in the city of Rome. As noted in Chapter 1, the Romans called their system a *rēspūblica*, or republic, from the Latin *rēs*, meaning thing or affair, and *pūblicus* or *pūblica*, meaning public—thus, a republic was the thing that belonged to the Roman people, the *populus romanus*.

Like Athens, Rome was originally a city-state. Although it expanded rapidly by conquest and annexation far beyond its original borders to encompass all the Mediterranean world and much of western Europe, its government remained, in its basic features, that of a moderately large city-state. Indeed, throughout the republican era (until roughly the end of the 1st century BCE), Roman assemblies were held in the very small Forum at the centre of the city.

Who constituted the Roman *dēmos?* Although Roman citizenship was conferred by birth, it was also granted by naturalization and by manumission of slaves. As the Roman Republic expanded, it conferred citizenship in varying degrees to many of those within its enlarged boundaries. Because Roman assemblies continued to meet in the Forum, however, most citizens who did not live in or near the city itself were unable to participate and were thus effectively excluded from the *dēmos.* Despite their reputation for practicality and creativity, and notwithstanding many changes in the structure of Roman government over the course of centuries, the Romans never solved this problem. Two millennia later, the solution—electing representatives to a Roman legislature—would seem obvious.

As they adapted to the special features of their society, including its rapidly increasing size, the Romans created a political structure so complex and idiosyncratic that later democratic leaders chose not to emulate it. The Romans used not only an extremely powerful Senate but also four assemblies, each called *comitia* ("assembly") or *concilium* ("council"). The Comitia Curiata was composed of 30 curiae, or local groups, drawn from three ancient *tribus*, or tribes; the Comitia Centuriata consisted of 193 centuries, or military units; the Concilium Plebis was drawn from the ranks of the plebes, or plebeians (common people); and the Comitia Tributa, like the Athenian Assembly, was open to all citizens. In all the assemblies, votes were counted by units (centuries or tribes) rather than by individuals; thus, insofar as a majority prevailed in voting, it would have been a majority of units, not of citizens.

Although they collectively represented all Roman citizens, the assemblies were not sovereign. Throughout the entire period of the republic, the Senate—an institution inherited from the earlier era of the Roman monarchy—continued to exercise great power. Senators were chosen

THE ROMAN SENATE

The Roman Senate, the governing and advisory council of ancient Rome, was the most permanent element in the Roman constitution. Under the Roman monarchy it served as an advisory council, with undefined powers. During the republic it advised the consuls and supposedly stood second to them in power. Senators were appointed by the consuls, but since they served for life, by the late republic the Senate became independent of the consuls, with extensive powers. About 312 BCE the selection of senators was transferred from the consuls to the censors. In 81 BCE the Roman dictator Lucius Cornelius Sulla made selection automatic, routinely admitting all former quaestors. It became the chief governing body and controlled the republic's finances. Julius Caesar increased the number of senators to 900. Augustus, the first Roman emperor, dropped the number to 300 and reduced the Senate's power, while giving it new judicial and legislative functions. The number later increased to about 2,000; many were provincials, the most important being the great landowners. The Senate's power faded until it disappeared from the historical record in the 6th century CE.

indirectly by the Comitia Centuriata; during the monarchy, they were drawn exclusively from the privileged patrician class, though later, during the republic, members of certain plebeian families were also admitted.

THE ITALIAN REPUBLICS FROM THE 12TH CENTURY TO THE RENAISSANCE

After the western Roman Empire collapsed in 476, the Italian Peninsula broke up into a congeries of smaller political entities. About six centuries later, in northern Italy, some of these entities developed into more or less independent city-states and inaugurated systems of government based on wider—though not fully popular—participation and on the election of leaders for limited periods of time. In this respect, their governments may be viewed as small-scale precursors of later representative systems. Such governments flourished for two centuries or more in a number of cities, including Venice, Florence, Siena, and Pisa.

"CONSTITUTIONAL OLIGARCHIES"

Drawing on Latin rather than Greek, the Italians called their city-states republics, not democracies. Although membership in the *dēmos* was at first restricted mainly to the nobility and large landowners, in some republics in the first half of the 13th century groups from lower social and economic classes—such as the newly rich, small merchants and bankers, skilled craftsmen organized in guilds, and foot soldiers commanded by knights—began to demand the right to participate in government at some level. Because they were more numerous than the upper classes and because they threatened (and sometimes carried out) violent uprisings, some of these groups were successful.

Even with these additions, however, the *dēmos* in the republics remained only a tiny fraction of the total population, ranging from 12 percent in 14th-century Bologna to 2 percent or less in 15th- and 16th-century Venice, where admission to the ruling nobility had been permanently closed during the 14th century. Thus, whether judged by the standards of Classical Greece or those of Europe and the United States in the 18th century and later, the Italian republics were not democracies. A more accurate characterization, proposed by the historian Lauro Martines, is "constitutional oligarchies."

After about the mid-14th century, the conditions that had favoured the existence of independent city-states and wider participation in government— particularly their economic growth and the civic loyalty of their populations—gradually disappeared. Economic decline, corruption, factional disputes, civil wars, and wars with other states led to the weakening of some republican governments and their eventual replacement by authoritarian rulers, whether monarchs, princes, or soldiers.

A DEMOCRATIC DILEMMA

The Greeks, the Romans, and the leaders of the Italian republics were pioneers in creating popular governments, and their philosophers and commentators exercised enormous influence on later political thought. Yet their political institutions were not emulated by the later founders of democratic governments in the nation-states of northern Europe and North America. As the expansion of Rome had already demonstrated, these institutions were simply not suited to political associations significantly larger than the city-state.

The enormous difference in size between a city-state and a nation-state points to a fundamental dilemma. By limiting the size of a city-state, citizens can in principle, if not always in practice, directly influence the conduct of their government—e.g., by participating in an assembly. But limiting size comes at a cost: important problems—notably defense against larger and more powerful states and the regulation of trade and finance—will remain beyond the capacity of the government to deal with effectively. Alternatively, by increasing the size of the city-state—i.e., by enlarging its geographic area and population—citizens can increase the capacity of the government to deal with important problems, but only at the cost of reducing their opportunities to influence the government directly through assemblies or other means.

Many city-states responded to this dilemma by forming alliances or confederations with other city-states and with larger political associations. But the problem would not finally be solved until the development of representative government, which first appeared in northern Europe in the 18th century.

CHAPTER 6
European and American Democracy to the End of the 19th Century

U ntil the 17th century, democratic theorists and political leaders largely ignored the possibility that a legislature might consist neither of the entire body of citizens, as in Greece and Rome, nor of representatives chosen by and from a tiny oligarchy or hereditary aristocracy, as in the Italian republics. An important break in the prevailing orthodoxy occurred during and after the English Civil Wars (1642–51), when the Levelers and other radical followers of Puritanism demanded broader representation in Parliament, expanded powers for Parliament's lower house, the House of Commons, and universal manhood suffrage. As with many political innovations, representative government resulted less from philosophical speculation than from a search for practical solutions to a fairly self-evident problem. Nevertheless, the complete assimilation of representation into the theory and practice of democracy was still more than a century away.

CONTINENTAL EUROPE

About 800 CE, freemen and nobles in various parts of northern Continental Europe began to participate directly in local assemblies, to which were later added regional and national assemblies consisting of representatives, some or all of whom came to be elected. In the mountain valleys of the Alps, such assemblies developed into self-governing cantons, leading eventually to the founding of the Swiss Confederation in the 13th century. By 900, local assemblies of Vikings were meeting in many areas of Scandinavia. Eventually the Vikings realized that to deal with certain larger problems they needed more-inclusive associations, and in Norway, Sweden, and Denmark regional assemblies developed. In 930 Viking descendants in Iceland created the first example of what today would be called a national assembly, legislature, or parliament—the Althing. In later centuries, representative institutions also were established in the emerging nation-states of Norway, Sweden, Denmark, Switzerland, and the Netherlands.

ENGLAND

Among the assemblies created in Europe during the Middle Ages, the one that most profoundly influenced the development of representative government was the English Parliament. Less a product of design than an unintended consequence of opportunistic innovations, Parliament grew out of councils that were called by kings for the purpose of redressing grievances and for exercising judicial functions. In time, Parliament began to deal with important matters of state, notably the raising of revenues needed to support the policies and decisions of the monarch. As its judicial functions were increasingly delegated to courts, it gradually evolved into a legislative body. By the end of the 15th century, the English system displayed some of the basic features of modern parliamentary government: for example, the enactment of laws now required the passage of bills by both houses of Parliament and the formal approval of the monarch.

Other important features had yet to be established, however. England's political life was dominated by the monarchy for centuries after the Middle Ages. During the English Civil Wars, led on one side by radical Puritans, the monarchy was abolished and a republic—the

A French depiction of the British king Charles's execution in 1649. With the king's death, the monarchy was abolished and the republic, known as the Commonwealth, was established. Hulton Archive/Getty Images

Commonwealth—was established (1649), though the monarchy was restored in 1660. By about 1800, significant powers, notably including powers related to the appointment and tenure of the prime minister, had shifted to Parliament. This development was strongly influenced by the emergence of political factions in Parliament during the early years of the 18th century. These factions, known as Whigs and Tories, later became full-fledged parties.

To king and Parliament alike it became increasingly apparent that laws could not be passed nor taxes raised without the support of a Whig or Tory leader who could muster a majority of votes in the House of Commons. To gain that support, the monarch was forced to select as prime minister the leader of the majority party in the Commons and to accept the leader's suggestions for the composition of the cabinet. That the monarch should have to yield to Parliament in this area became manifest during a constitutional crisis in 1782, when King George III (reigned 1760–1820) was compelled, much against his will, to accept a Whig prime minister and cabinet—a situation he regarded, according to one scholar, as "a violation of the Constitution, a defeat for his policy, and a personal humiliation." By 1830 the constitutional principle that the choice of prime minister, and thus the cabinet, reposed with the House of Commons had become firmly entrenched in the (unwritten) British Constitution.

Parliamentary government in Britain was not yet a democratic system, however. Mainly because of property requirements, the franchise was held by only about 5 percent of the British population over 20 years of age. The Reform Act of 1832, which is generally viewed as a historic threshold in the development of parliamentary democracy in Britain, extended the suffrage to about 7 percent of the adult population. It would require further acts of Parliament in 1867, 1884, and 1918 to achieve universal male suffrage and one more law, enacted in 1928, to secure the right to vote for all adult women.

THE UNITED STATES

Whereas the feasibility of representative government was demonstrated by the development of Parliament, the possibility of joining representation with democracy first became fully evident in the governments of the British colonies of North America and later in the founding of the United States of America.

Conditions in colonial America favoured the limited development of a system of representation more broadly based than the one in use in Great Britain. These conditions included the vast distance from London, which

forced the British government to grant significant autonomy to the colonies; the existence of colonial legislatures
in which representatives in at least one house were elected
by voters; the expansion of the suffrage, which in some
colonies came to include most adult white males; the
spread of property ownership, particularly in land; and the
strengthening of beliefs in fundamental rights and popular sovereignty, including the belief that the colonists, as
British citizens, should not have to pay taxes to a government in which they were not represented ("no taxation
without representation").

Until about 1760, most colonists were loyal to the
mother country and did not think of themselves as con-
stituting a separate nation of "Americans." After Britain
imposed direct taxation on the colonies through the
Stamp Act (1765), however, there were public (and sometimes violent) displays of opposition to the new law.
In colonial newspapers there was also a sharp increase
in the use of the term *Americans* to refer to the colonial
population. Other factors that helped to create a distinct
American identity were the outbreak of war with Britain
in 1775 and the shared hardships and suffering of the
people during many years of fighting, the adoption of the
Declaration of Independence in 1776, the flight of many
loyalists to Canada and England, and the rapid increase in
travel and communication between the newly independent states. The colonists' sense of themselves as a single
people, fragile as it may have been, made possible the creation of a loose confederacy of states under the Articles of
Confederation in 1781–89 and an even more unified federal government under the Constitution in 1789.

Because of the new country's large population and
enormous size, it was obvious to the delegates to the
Constitutional Convention (1787) that "the People of the
United States," as the opening words of the Constitution

referred to them, could govern themselves at the federal level only by electing representatives—a practice with which the delegates were already familiar, given their experience of state government and, more remotely, their dealings with the government in Britain. The new representative government was barely in place, however, when it became evident that the task of organizing members of Congress and the electorate required the existence of political parties, even though such parties had been regarded as pernicious and destructive—"the bane of republics"—by political thinkers and by many delegates to the Constitutional Convention. Eventually, political parties in the United States would provide nominees for local, state, and national offices and compete openly and vigorously in elections.

THE CONSTITUTIONAL CONVENTION

The Constitutional Convention was the body that in 1787 drew up the Constitution of the United States. Stimulated by severe economic troubles, which produced radical political movements such as Shays's Rebellion, and urged on by a demand for a stronger central government, the convention met in the Pennsylvania State House in Philadelphia (May 25–Sept. 17, 1787), ostensibly to amend the Articles of Confederation. All the states except Rhode Island responded to an invitation issued by the Annapolis Convention of 1786 to send delegates. Of the 74 deputies chosen by the state legislatures, only 55 took part in the proceedings; of these, 39 signed the Constitution. The delegates included many of the leading figures of the period. Among them were George Washington, who was elected to preside, James Madison, Benjamin Franklin, James Wilson, John Rutledge, Charles Pinckney, Oliver Ellsworth, and Gouverneur Morris.

Discarding the idea of amending the Articles of Confederation, the assembly set about drawing up a new scheme of government but found itself divided, delegates from small states (those without claims to unoccupied western lands) opposing those from large states over the apportionment of representation. Edmund Randolph offered a plan known as the Virginia, or large state, plan, which provided for a bicameral legislature with representation of each state based on its population or wealth. William Paterson proposed the New Jersey, or small state, plan, which provided for equal representation in Congress. Neither the large nor the small states would yield. Oliver Ellsworth and Roger Sherman, among others, in what is sometimes called the Connecticut, or Great, Compromise, proposed a bicameral legislature with proportional representation in the lower house and equal representation of the states in the upper house. All revenue measures would originate in the lower house. That compromise was approved July 16.

The matter of counting slaves in the population for figuring representation was settled by a compromise agreement that three-fifths of the slaves should be counted as population in apportioning representation and should also be counted as property in assessing taxes. Controversy over the abolition of the importation of slaves ended with the agreement that importation should not be forbidden before 1808. The powers of the federal executive and judiciary were enumerated, and the Constitution was itself declared to be the "supreme law of the land." The convention's work was approved by a majority of the states the following year.

It was also obvious that a country as large as the United States would require representative government at lower levels—e.g., territories, states, and municipalities—with correspondingly limited powers. Although the governments of territories and states were necessarily representative, in smaller associations a direct assembly of citizens was both feasible and desirable. In many New England towns, for example, citizens assembled in meetings, Athenian style, to discuss and vote on local matters.

Thus, the citizens of the United States helped to provide new answers to question (1)—What is the appropriate unit or association within which a democratic government should be established?—and to question (3)—How are citizens to govern? Yet, the American answer to question (2)—Who should constitute the *dēmos?*—though radical in its time, was by later standards highly unsatisfactory. Even as the suffrage was broadly extended among adult white males, it continued to exclude large segments of the adult population, such as women, slaves, many freed blacks, and Native Americans. In time, these exclusions, like those of earlier democracies and republics, would be widely regarded as undemocratic.

DEMOCRACY OR REPUBLIC?

Is *democracy* the most appropriate name for a large-scale representative system such as that of the early United States? At the end of the 18th century, the history of the terms whose literal meaning is "rule by the people"—*democracy* and *republic*—left the answer unclear. Both terms had been applied to the assembly-based systems of Greece and Rome, though neither system assigned legislative powers to representatives elected by members of the *dēmos.* As noted above, even after Roman citizenship was expanded beyond the city itself and increasing numbers of citizens were prevented from participating in government by the time, expense, and hardship of travel to the city, the complex Roman system of assemblies was never replaced by a government of representatives—a parliament—elected by all Roman citizens. Venetians also called the government of their famous city a republic, though it was certainly not democratic.

When the members of the United States Constitutional Convention met in 1787, terminology was still unsettled. Not only were *democracy* and *republic* used more or less interchangeably in the colonies, but no established term existed for a representative government "by the people." At the same time, the British system was moving swiftly toward full-fledged parliamentary government. Had the framers of the United States Constitution met two generations later, when their understanding of the constitution of Britain would have been radically different, they might have concluded that the British system required only an expansion of the electorate to realize its full democratic potential. Thus, they might well have adopted a parliamentary form of government.

Embarked as they were on a wholly unprecedented effort to construct a constitutional government for an already large and continuously expanding country, the framers could have had no clear idea of how their experiment would work in practice. Fearful of the destructive power of "factions," for example, they did not foresee that in a country where laws are enacted by representatives chosen by the people in regular and competitive elections, political parties inevitably become fundamentally important institutions.

Given the existing confusion over terminology, it is not surprising that the framers employed various terms to describe the novel government they proposed. A few months after the adjournment of the Constitutional Convention, James Madison, the future fourth president of the United States, proposed a usage that would have lasting influence within the country though little elsewhere. In "Federalist 10," one of 85 essays by Madison,

Alexander Hamilton, and John Jay known collectively as the Federalist Papers, Madison defined a "pure democracy" as "a society consisting of a small number of citizens, who assemble and administer the government in person," and a republic as "a government in which the scheme of representation takes place." According to Madison, "The two great points of difference between a democracy and a republic, are: first, the delegation of the government, in the latter, to a small number of citizens elected by the rest; secondly, the greater the number of citizens, and greater sphere of country, over which the latter may be extended." In short, for Madison, *democracy* meant direct democracy, and *republic* meant representative government.

Even among his contemporaries, Madison's refusal to apply the term *democracy* to representative governments, even those based on broad electorates, was aberrant. In November 1787, only two months after the convention had adjourned, James Wilson, one of the signers of the Declaration of Independence, proposed a new classification. "[T]he three species of governments," he wrote, "are the monarchical, aristocratical and democratical. In a monarchy, the supreme power is vested in a single person: in an aristocracy... by a body not formed

James Madison. In the Federalist Papers, Madison took pains to differentiate between a republic and a democracy. Jack Zehrt/Taxi/Getty Images

upon the principle of representation, but enjoying their station by descent, or election among themselves, or in right of some personal or territorial qualifications; and lastly, in a democracy, it is inherent in a people, and is exercised by themselves or their representatives." Applying this understanding of democracy to the newly adopted constitution, Wilson asserted that "in its principles, ... it is purely democratical: varying indeed in its form in order to admit all the advantages, and to exclude all the disadvantages which are incidental to the known and established constitutions of government. But when we take an extensive and accurate view of the streams of power that appear through this great and comprehensive plan...we shall be able to trace them to one great and noble source, THE PEOPLE." At the Virginia ratifying convention some months later, John Marshall, the future chief justice of the Supreme Court, declared that the "Constitution provided for 'a well regulated democracy' where no king, or president, could undermine representative government." The political party that he helped to organize and lead in cooperation with Thomas Jefferson, principal author of the Declaration of Independence and future third president of the United States, was named the Democratic-Republican Party; the party adopted its present name, the Democratic Party, in 1844.

Following his visit to the United States in 1831–32, the French political scientist Alexis de Tocqueville asserted in no uncertain terms that the country he had observed was a democracy—indeed, the world's first representative democracy, where the fundamental principle of government was "the sovereignty of the people." Tocqueville's estimation of the American system of government reached a wide audience in Europe and beyond through his monumental four-volume study *Democracy in America* (1835–40).

SOLVING THE DILEMMA

Thus, by the end of the 18th century both the idea and the practice of democracy had been profoundly transformed. Political theorists and statesmen now recognized what the Levelers had seen earlier, that the nondemocratic practice of representation could be used to make democracy practicable in the large nation-states of the modern era. Representation, in other words, was the solution to the ancient dilemma between enhancing the ability of political associations to deal with large-scale problems and preserving the opportunity of citizens to participate in government.

To some of those steeped in the older tradition, the union of representation and democracy seemed a marvelous and epochal invention. In the early 19th century the French author Destutt de Tracy, the inventor of the term *idéologie* ("ideology"), insisted that representation had rendered obsolete the doctrines of both Montesquieu and Jean-Jacques Rousseau, both of whom had denied that representative governments could be genuinely democratic. "Representation, or representative government," he wrote, "may be considered as a new invention, unknown in Montesquieu's time.... Representative democracy ... is democracy rendered practicable for a long time and over a great extent of territory." In 1820 the English philosopher James Mill proclaimed "the system of representation" to be "the grand discovery of modern times" in which "the solution of all the difficulties, both speculative and practical, will perhaps be found." One generation later Mill's son, the philosopher John Stuart Mill, concluded in his *Considerations on Representative Government* (1861) that "the ideal type of a perfect government" would be both democratic and representative. Foreshadowing developments that would take place in the 20th century, the *dēmos* of Mill's representative democracy included women.

NEW ANSWERS TO OLD QUESTIONS

Representation was not the only radical innovation in democratic ideas and institutions. Equally revolutionary were the new answers being offered, in the 19th and 20th centuries, to some of the fundamental questions mentioned earlier.

SUFFRAGE

One important development concerned question (2)— Who should constitute the *dēmos?* In the 19th century property requirements for voting were reduced and finally removed. The exclusion of women from the *dēmos* was increasingly challenged—not least by women themselves. Beginning with New Zealand in 1893, more and more countries granted women the suffrage and other political rights, and by the mid-20th century women were full and equal members of the *dēmos* in almost all countries that considered themselves democratic—though Switzerland, a pioneer in establishing universal male suffrage in 1848, did not grant women the right to vote in national elections until 1971.

Although the United States granted women the right to vote in 1920, another important exclusion continued for almost half a century: African Americans were prevented, by both legal and illegal means, from voting and other forms of political activity, primarily in the South but also in other areas of the country. Not until after the passage and vigorous enforcement of the Civil Rights Act of 1964 were they at last effectively admitted into the American *dēmos*.

Thus, in the 19th and 20th centuries the *dēmos* was gradually expanded to include all adult citizens. Although important issues remained unsettled—for example, should permanent legal foreign residents of a country be entitled to vote?—such an expanded _dēmos_ became a new condition of democracy itself. By the mid-20th century, no system whose _dēmos_ did not include all adult citizens could properly be called "democratic."

FACTIONS AND PARTIES

In many of the city-state democracies and republics, part of the answer to question (3)—What political institutions are necessary for governing?—consisted of "factions," including both informal groups and organized political parties. Much later, representative democracies in several countries developed political parties for selecting candidates for election to parliament and for organizing parliamentary support for (or opposition to) the prime minister and his cabinet. Nevertheless, at the end of the 18th century leading political theorists such as Montesquieu continued to regard factions as a profound danger to democracies and republics. This view was also common at the United States Constitutional Convention, where many delegates argued that the new government would inevitably be controlled and abused by factions unless there existed a strong system of constitutional checks and balances.

Factions are dangerous, it was argued, for at least two reasons. First, a faction is by definition a group whose interests are in conflict with the general good. As Madison put it in "Federalist 10": "By a faction, I understand a number of citizens, whether amounting to a majority or a minority of the whole, who are united and actuated by some common impulse of passion, or of interest, adverse to the rights of other citizens, or to the permanent and aggregate interests of the community." Second, historical experience shows that, prior to the 18th century, the existence of factions in a democracy or republic tended to undermine the stability of its government. The "insta-bility, injustice, and confusion introduced into the public councils" by factionalism, Madison wrote, have been "the mortal diseases under which popular governments have everywhere perished."

Interestingly, Madison used the presumed danger of factions as an argument in favour of adopting the new constitution. Because the United States, in comparison with previous republics, would have many more citizens and vastly more territory, the diversity of interests among its population would be much greater, making the forma-tion of large or powerful factions less likely. Similarly, the exercise of government power by representatives rather than directly by the people would "refine and enlarge the public views, by passing them through the medium of a chosen body of citizens, whose wisdom may best discern the true interest of their country."

As to political parties, Madison soon realized—despite his belief in the essential perniciousness of factions—that in a representative democracy political parties are not only legally possible, necessary, and inevitable, they are also desirable. They were legally possible because of the rights and liberties provided for in the constitution. They were necessary in order to defeat the Federalists, whose centralizing policies Madison, Jefferson, and many others strongly opposed. Because parties were both possible and necessary, they would inevitably be created. Finally, par-ties were also desirable, because by helping to mobilize voters throughout the country and in the legislative body, they enabled the majority to prevail over the opposition of a minority.

This view came to be shared by political thinkers in other countries in which democratic forms of govern-ment were developing. By the end of the 19th century, it was nearly universally accepted that the existence of

independent and competitive political parties is an ele-
mentary standard that every democracy must meet.

MAJORITY RULE, MINORITY RIGHTS, MAJORITY TYRANNY

The fear of "majority tyranny" was a common theme in the
17th century and later, even among those who were sympa-
thetic to democracy. Given the opportunity, it was argued,
a majority would surely trample on the fundamental rights
of minorities. Property rights were perceived as particularly vulnerable, since presumably any majority of citizens
with little or no property would be tempted to infringe
the rights of the propertied minority. Such concerns were
shared by Madison and other delegates at the convention
and strongly influenced the document they created.

Here, too, however, Madison's views changed after
reflection on and observation of the emerging American
democracy. In a letter of 1833, he wrote, "[E]very friend
to Republican government ought to raise his voice against
the sweeping denunciation of majority governments as
the most tyrannical and intolerable of all governments....
[N]o government of human device and human administration can be perfect; ... the abuses of all other governments
have led to the preference of republican government as
the best of all governments, because the least imperfect;
[and] the vital principle of republican governments is the
lex majoris partis, the will of the majority."

The fear of factions was eased and finally abandoned
after leaders in various democratic countries realized that
they could create numerous barriers to unrestrained majority rule, none of which would be clearly inconsistent with
basic democratic principles. Thus, they could incorporate
a bill of rights into the constitution; require a superma-
jority of votes—such as two-thirds or three-fourths—for

constitutional amendments and other important kinds of legislation; divide the executive, legislative, and judicial powers of government into separate branches; give an independent judiciary the power to declare laws or policies unconstitutional and hence without force of law; adopt constitutional guarantees of significant autonomy for states, provinces, or regions; provide by statute for the decentralization of government to territorial groups such as towns, counties, and cities; or adopt a system of proportional representation, under which the proportion of legislative seats awarded to a party is roughly the same as the proportion of votes cast for the party or its candidates. In such a multiparty system, cabinets are composed of representatives drawn from two or more parties, thus ensuring that minority interests retain a significant voice in government.

Although political theorists continue to disagree about the best means to effect majority rule in democratic systems, it seems evident that majorities cannot legitimately abridge the fundamental rights of citizens. Nor should minorities ever be entitled to prevent the enforcement of laws and policies designed to protect these fundamental rights. In short, because democracy is not only a political system of "rule by the people" but necessarily also a system of rights, a government that infringes these rights is to that extent undemocratic.

CHAPTER 7

Democracy in the 20th and 21st Centuries

During the 20th century, the number of countries possessing the basic political institutions of representative democracy increased significantly. At the beginning of the 21st century, independent observers agreed that more than one-third of the world's nominally independent countries possessed democratic institutions comparable to those of the English-speaking countries and the older democracies of Continental Europe. In an additional one-sixth of the world's countries, these institutions, though somewhat flawed, nevertheless provided historically high levels of democratic government. Altogether, these democratic and near-democratic countries contained nearly half the world's population. What accounted for this rapid expansion of democratic institutions?

FAILURES OF NONDEMOCRATIC SYSTEMS

A significant part of the explanation is that all the main alternatives to democracy—whether of ancient or of modern origins—suffered political, economic, diplomatic, and military failures that greatly lessened their appeal. With the victory of the Allies in World War I, the ancient systems of monarchy, aristocracy, and oligarchy ceased to be legitimate. Following the military defeat of Italy and Germany in World War II, the newer alternative of fascism was likewise discredited, as was Soviet-style communism after the dissolution of the Soviet Union in 1991. Similar

Protestors in 1988 Moscow, some of whom were rallying in favor of Glastnost for Soviet-controlled Nagorno-Karabakh. A policy of governmental openness, Glasnost marked the beginning of democratization in the former Soviet Union. Vitaly Armand/AFP/Getty Images

failures contributed to the gradual disappearance of military dictatorships in Latin America in the 1980s and '90s.

MARKET ECONOMIES

Accompanying these ideological and institutional changes were changes in economic institutions. Highly centralized economies under state control had enabled political leaders to use their ready access to economic resources to reward their allies and punish their critics. As these systems were displaced by more decentralized market economies, the power and influence of top government officials declined. In addition, some of the conditions that were essential to the successful functioning of market economies also contributed to the development of democracy: ready access to reliable information, relatively high levels of education, ease of personal movement, and the rule of law. As market economies expanded and as middle classes grew larger and more influential, popular support for such conditions increased, often accompanied by demands for further democratization.

ECONOMIC WELL-BEING

The development of market economies contributed to the spread of democracy in other ways as well. As the economic well-being of large segments of the world's population gradually improved, so, too, did the likelihood that newly established democratic institutions would survive and flourish. In general, citizens in democratic countries

Haitian citizens demonstrate against American and United Nations intervention outside the U.S. Embassy in Port-au-Prince in 1993. At the time the impoverished nation was under the control of an antidemocratic military regime. Bob Pearson/AFP/Getty Images

with persistent poverty are more susceptible to the appeals of antidemocratic demagogues who promise simple and immediate solutions to their country's economic problems. Accordingly, widespread economic prosperity in a country greatly increases the chances that democratic government will succeed, whereas widespread poverty greatly increases the chances that it will fail.

POLITICAL CULTURE

During the 20th century, democracy continued to exist in some countries despite periods of acute diplomatic, military, economic, or political crisis, such as occurred during the early years of the Great Depression. The survival of democratic institutions in these countries is attributable in part to the existence in their societies of a culture of widely shared democratic beliefs and values. Such attitudes are acquired early in life from older generations, thus becoming embedded in people's views of themselves, their country, and the world. In countries where democratic culture is weak or absent, as was the case in the Weimar Republic of Germany in the years following World War I, democracy is much more vulnerable, and periods of crisis are more likely to lead to a reversion to a nondemocratic regime.

CONTEMPORARY DEMOCRATIC SYSTEMS

Differences among democratic countries in historical experience, size, ethnic and religious composition, and other factors have resulted in significant differences in their political institutions. Some of the features with respect to which these institutions have differed are the following.

PRESIDENTIAL AND PARLIAMENTARY SYSTEMS

Whereas versions of the American presidential system were frequently adopted in Latin America, Africa, and elsewhere in the developing world (where the military sometimes converted the office into a dictatorship through a coup d'état), as European countries democratized they adopted versions of the English parliamentary system, which made use of both a prime minister responsible to parliament and a ceremonial head of state. The latter person might be either a hereditary monarch, as in the Scandinavian countries, the Netherlands, and Spain, or a president chosen by parliament or by another body convoked specially for the purpose. A notable exception is France, which in its fifth constitution, adopted in 1958, combined its parliamentary system with a presidential one.

UNITARY AND FEDERAL SYSTEMS

In most older European and English-speaking democracies, political authority inheres in the central government, which is constitutionally authorized to determine the limited powers, as well as the geographic boundaries, of subnational associations such as states and regions. Such unitary systems contrast markedly with federal systems, in which authority is constitutionally divided between the central government and the governments of relatively autonomous subnational entities. Democratic countries that have adopted federal systems include—in addition to the United States—Switzerland, Germany, Austria, Spain, Canada, and Australia. The world's most populous democratic country, India, also has a federal system.

PROPORTIONAL AND WINNER-TAKE-ALL SYSTEMS

Electoral arrangements vary enormously. Some democratic countries divide their territories into electoral districts, each of which is entitled to a single seat in the legislature, the seat being won by the candidate who gains the most votes—hence the terms *first past the post* in Britain and *winner take all* in the United States. As critics of this system point out, in districts contested by more than two candidates, it is possible to gain the seat with less than a strict majority of votes (50 percent plus one). As a result, a party that receives only a minority of votes in the entire country could win a majority of seats in the legislature. Systems of proportional representation are designed to ensure a closer correspondence between the proportion of votes cast for a party and the proportion of seats it receives. With few exceptions, Continental European countries have adopted some form of proportional representation, as have Ireland, Australia, New Zealand, Japan, and South Korea. Winner-take-all systems remain in the United States, Canada, and, for parliamentary elections, in Britain.

TWO-PARTY AND MULTIPARTY SYSTEMS

Because proportional representation does not favour large parties over smaller ones, as does the winner-take-all system, in countries with proportional representation there are almost always three or more parties represented in the legislature, and a coalition government consisting of two or more parties is ordinarily necessary to win legislative support for the government's policies. Thus the prevalence of proportional representation effectively ensures that coalition governments are the rule in democratic countries; governments consisting of only two parties, such as that of the United States, are extremely rare.

MAJORITARIAN AND CONSENSUAL SYSTEMS

Because of differences in electoral systems and other factors, democratic countries differ with respect to whether laws and policies can be enacted by a single, relatively cohesive party with a legislative majority, as is ordinarily the case in Britain and Japan, or instead require consensus among several parties with diverse views, as in Switzerland, the Netherlands, Sweden, Italy, and elsewhere. Political scientists and others disagree about which of the two types of system, majoritarian or consensual, is more desirable. Critics of consensual systems argue that they allow a minority of citizens to veto policies they dislike and that they make the tasks of forming governments and passing legislation excessively difficult. Supporters contend that consensual arrangements produce comparatively wider public support for government policies and even help to increase the legitimacy and perceived value of democracy itself.

Here again, it appears that a country's basic political institutions need to be tailored to its particular conditions and historical experience. The strongly majoritarian system of Britain would probably be inappropriate in Switzerland, whereas the consensual arrangements of Switzerland or the Netherlands might be less satisfactory in Britain.

CONTEMPORARY CHALLENGES

At the beginning of the 21st century, democracy faced a number of challenges, some of which had been problems of long standing, others of which were of more recent origin.

INEQUALITY OF RESOURCES

Although decentralized market economies encouraged the spread of democracy, in countries where they were not sufficiently regulated, such economies eventually produced large inequalities in economic and social resources, from wealth and income to education and social status. Because those with greater resources naturally tended to use them to influence the political system to their advantage, the existence of such inequalities constituted a persistent obstacle to the achievement of a satisfactory level of political equality. This challenge was magnified during regularly occurring economic downturns, when poverty and unemployment tended to increase.

IMMIGRATION

After World War II, immigration to the countries of western Europe, Australia, and the United States, both legal and illegal, increased dramatically. Seeking to escape poverty or oppression in their homelands and usually lacking education, immigrants primarily from the developing world typically took menial jobs in service industries or agriculture. Differences in language, culture, and appearance between immigrant groups and the citizens of the host country, as well as the usually widespread perception that immigrants take jobs away from citizens and use expensive social services, made immigration a hotly debated issue in many countries.

In some instances, anti-immigrant sentiment contributed to the rise of radical political parties and movements, such as the National Front in France, the Republicans in Germany, the militia movement in the United States, and the skinhead movement in the United States and Britain. Some of these groups promoted racist or neofascist

People rallying at the Arizona state capitol in 2010, protesting for and against the enactment of stricter immigration laws. Immigration has been a political hot-button issue for decades. John Moore/Getty Images

doctrines that were hostile not only to immigrants but also to fundamental political and human rights and even to democracy itself.

TERRORISM

Acts of terrorism committed within democratic countries or against their interests in other parts of the world occurred with increasing frequency beginning in the 1970s. In the United States remarkably few terrorist attacks had taken place before the 1993 bombing of the World Trade Center in New York City. The deadliest single act of terrorism anywhere, the September 11 attacks of 2001, destroyed the World Trade Center and killed some 3,000 people, mainly in New York City and Washington, D.C. Subsequent significant terrorist acts in democratic countries included the bombings of commuter trains in Madrid in March 2004, the suicide bombings of the London transit system in July 2005, and the attacks by gunmen on sites in Mumbai in November 2008.

In response to such events, and especially in the wake of the September 11 attacks, democratic governments adopted various measures designed to enhance the ability of police and other law-enforcement agencies to protect their countries against terrorism. Some of these initiatives entailed new restrictions on citizens' civil and political liberties and were accordingly criticized as unconstitutional

THE SEPTEMBER 11 ATTACKS

The September 11 attacks were a series of airline hijackings and suicide bombings in the U.S. perpetrated by 19 militants associated with the Islamic extremist group al-Qaeda. The attacks were planned well in advance; the militants—most of whom were from Saudi Arabia—traveled to the U.S. beforehand, where a number received commercial flight training. Working in small groups, the hijackers boarded four domestic airliners in groups of five (a 20th participant was alleged) on Sept. 11, 2001, and took control of the planes soon after takeoff. At 8:46 a.m. (local time), the terrorists piloted the first plane into the north tower of the World Trade Center in New York City. A second plane struck the south tower some 15 minutes later. Both structures erupted in flames and, badly damaged, soon collapsed. A third plane struck the southwest side of the Pentagon near Washington, D.C., at 9:40 a.m., and within the next hour the fourth crashed in Pennsylvania after its passengers, aware of events via cellular telephone, attempted to overpower their assailants. Some 2,750 people were killed in New York, 184 at the Pentagon, and 40 in Pennsylvania. All 19 terrorists died.

or otherwise inconsistent with democratic principles. In the early 21st century it remained to be seen whether democratic governments could strike a satisfactory balance between the sometimes conflicting imperatives of ensuring security and preserving democracy.

INTERNATIONAL SYSTEMS

At the end of the 18th century, in response to the dilemma of size described earlier, the focus of both the theory and the practice of democracy shifted from the small association of the city-state to the far larger nation-state. Although their increased size enabled democracies to solve more of the problems they confronted, there remained some problems that not even the largest democracy could solve by itself. To address these problems several international organizations were established after World War II, most notably the United Nations (1945), and their numbers and responsibilities grew rapidly through the rest of the 20th century.

These organizations posed two related challenges to democracy. First, by shifting ultimate control of a country's policies in a certain area to the international level, they reduced to a corresponding extent the influence that citizens could exert on such policies through democratic means. Second, all international organizations, even those that were formally accountable to national governments, lacked the political institutions of representative democracy. How could these institutions be made democratic—or at least more democratic?

In their struggle to forge a constitution for the new European Union at the beginning of the 21st century, European leaders faced both of these challenges, as well as most of the fundamental questions posed in Chapter 5.

What kind of association is appropriate to a democratic government of Europe? What persons or entities should constitute the European *dēmos?* What political organizations or institutions are needed? Should decisions be made by majority? If so, by what kind of majority—a majority of persons, of countries, of both countries and persons, or of something else? Do all the conditions necessary for satisfactory democratic government exist in this huge and diverse association? If not, would a less-democratic system be more desirable?

CHAPTER 8

The Theory of Democracy from Pericles to Rawls

The development of democratic political institutions has been influenced by philosophical speculation concerning the justification of political authority, the rights and liberties of individuals, the qualities of human nature, and the "human good"—that which is necessary for, or constitutive of, human flourishing. During the European Enlightenment the democratic political theories of John Locke and Montesquieu provided inspiration and even a vocabulary for the great revolutions that established democratic government in the new United States and overthrew absolutist monarchy in France. During subsequent periods much political philosophy and political theory in the English-speaking world has been devoted to exploring the concept of democracy and examining its implications for the moral evaluation of actually existing political institutions.

PERICLES

In a funeral oration in 430 BCE for those who had fallen in the Peloponnesian War, the Athenian leader Pericles described democratic Athens as "the school of Hellas." Among the city's many exemplary qualities, he declared, was its constitution, which "favors the many instead of the few; this is why it is called a democracy." Pericles continued: "If we look to the laws, they afford equal justice to all in their private differences; if to social standing, advancement in public life falls to reputation for capacity, class considerations not being allowed to interfere with merit; nor again does poverty bar the way; if a man is able to serve the state, he is not hindered by obscurity of his condition. The freedom which we enjoy in our government extends also to our ordinary life."

ARISTOTLE

A century later, Aristotle discussed democracy in terms that would become highly influential in comparative studies of political systems. At the heart of his approach is the notion of a "constitution," which he defines as "an organization of offices, which all the citizens distribute among themselves, according to the power which different classes possess." He concludes that "there must therefore be as many forms of government as there are modes of arranging the offices, according to the superiorities and the differences of the parts of the state." Ever the realist, however, he remarks that "the best [government] is often unattainable, and therefore the true legislator and statesman ought to be acquainted, not only with (1) that which is best in the abstract, but also with (2) that which is best relatively to circumstances."

Aristotle identifies three kinds of ideal constitution—each of which describes a situation in which those who rule pursue the common good—and three corresponding kinds of perverted constitution—each of which describes a situation in which those who rule pursue narrow and selfish goals. The three kinds of constitution, both ideal and perverted, are differentiated by the number of persons they allow to rule. Thus "rule by one" is monarchy in its ideal form and tyranny in its perverted form; "rule by the few" is aristocracy in its ideal form and oligarchy in its perverted form; and "rule by the many" is "polity" in its ideal form and democracy in its perverted form.

Portrait of the Greek philosopher Aristotle by Antonio Maria Crespi. DEA/Veneranda Biblioteca Ambrosiana/Getty Images

Aristotle's general scheme prevailed for more than two millennia, though his unsympathetic and puzzling definition of democracy—which probably did not reflect the views of most Greeks in his time—did not. Aristotle himself took a more favourable view of democracy in his studies of the variety, stability, and composition of actual democratic governments. In his observation that "the basis of a democratic state is liberty," Aristotle proposed a connection between the ideas of democracy and liberty that would be strongly emphasized by all later advocates of democracy.

JOHN LOCKE

Nearly 20 centuries after Aristotle, the English philosopher John Locke adopted the essential elements of the Aristotelian classification of constitutions in his *Second Treatise of Civil Government* (1690). Unlike Aristotle, however, Locke was an unequivocal supporter of political equality, individual liberty, democracy, and majority rule. Although his work was naturally rather abstract and not particularly programmatic, it provided a powerful philosophical foundation for much later democratic theorizing and political programs.

THE LEGITIMACY OF GOVERNMENT

According to Locke, in the hypothetical "state of nature" that precedes the creation of human societies, men live "equal one amongst another without subordination or subjection," and they are perfectly free to act and to dispose of their possessions as they see fit, within the bounds of natural law. From these and other premises Locke draws the conclusion that political society—i.e., government—insofar as it is legitimate, represents a social contract among those who have "consented to make one Community or Government ... wherein the Majority have a right to act and conclude the rest." These two ideas—the consent of the governed and majority rule—became central to all subsequent theories of democracy. For Locke they are inextricably connected: "For if the consent of the majority shall not in reason, be received, as the act of the whole, and conclude every individual; nothing but the consent of every individual can make anything be the act of the whole: But such a consent is next to impossible ever to be had." Thus no government is legitimate unless it enjoys the consent of the governed, and that consent cannot be rendered except through majority rule.

Given these conclusions, it is somewhat surprising that Locke's description of the different forms of government (he calls them "commonwealths") does not explicitly prescribe democracy as the only legitimate system. Writing in England in the 1680s, a generation after the Commonwealth ended with the restoration of the monarchy (1660), Locke was more circumspect than this. Nevertheless, a careful reading of the relevant passages of the *Second Treatise* shows that Locke remains true to his fundamental principle, that the only legitimate

Among the political conceits espoused by English philosopher John Locke were equality and the rights of the governed. Hulton Archvie/Getty Images

form of government is that based on the consent of the governed.

Locke differentiates the various forms of government on the basis of where the people choose to place the power to make laws. His categories are the traditional ones: If the people retain the legislative power for themselves, together with the power to appoint those who execute the laws, then "the Form of the Government is a perfect Democracy." If they put the power "into the hands of a few select Men, and their Heirs or Successors,...then it is an Oligarchy: Or else into the hands of one Man, and then it is a Monarchy." Nevertheless, his analysis is far more subversive of nondemocratic forms of government than it appears to be. For whatever the form of government, the ultimate source of sovereign power is the people, and all legitimate government must rest on their consent. Therefore, if a government abuses its trust and violates the people's fundamental rights—particularly the right to property—the people are entitled to rebel and replace that government with another to whose laws they can willingly give their consent. And who is to judge whether the government has abused its trust? Again, Locke is unequivocal: the people themselves are to make that judgment. Although he does not use the term, Locke thus unambiguously affirms the right of revolution against a despotic government.

Less than a century later, Locke's views were echoed in the famous words of the United States Declaration of Independence:

> *We hold these truths to be self-evident, that all men are created equal, that they are endowed by their Creator with certain unalienable Rights, that among these are Life, Liberty, and the pursuit of Happiness. That to secure these rights, Governments*

*are instituted among Men, deriving their just pow-
ers from the consent of the governed, that whenever
any Form of Government becomes destructive of
these ends, it is the Right of the People to alter or
abolish it, and to institute new government, laying
its foundation on such principles and organizing its
powers in such form, as to them shall seem most likely
to effect their Safety and Happiness.*

ANSWERS TO FUNDAMENTAL QUESTIONS

Although Locke's ideas were radical—even quietly revolutionary—in his time, his answers to the first three
questions posed in Chapter 5 would need further elabora-
tion, and even some alteration, as the theory and practice
of democracy continued to develop.

Regarding question (1)—What is the appropriate association within which a democratic government should
be established?—despite the generality of his conclusions, Locke clearly intended them to apply to England
as a whole, and presumably also to other nation-states.
Departing from views that still prevailed among political philosophers of his time, Locke held—as the Levelers
did—that democracy did not require a small political unit,
such as a city-state, in which all members of the *dēmos* could
participate in government directly. Here again, Locke was
at the forefront of the development of democratic ideas.

Regarding question (2)—Who should constitute the
dēmos?—Locke believed, along with almost everyone else
who had expressed an opinion on the issue, that children
should not enjoy the full rights of citizenship, though he
maintained that parents are morally obliged to respect
their children's rights as human beings. With almost no
substantive argument, Locke adopted the traditional view
that women should be excluded from the *dēmos*, though

he insisted that they retain all other fundamental rights. More than a century would pass before "the consent of the people" was generally understood to include the consent of women.

Unlike the men of Athens or the small male aristocracy of Venice, obviously the men of England could not govern directly in an assembly. In this case, then, the answer to question (3)—What political institutions are necessary for governing?—would have to include the use of representatives chosen by the people. Yet, though it seems clear that Locke's government by consent requires representation, he provided little guidance as to the form it might take. This is perhaps because he, like his contemporary readers, assumed that democracy and majority rule would be best implemented in England through parliamentary elections based on an adult-male franchise.

MONTESQUIEU

The French political theorist Montesquieu, through his masterpiece *The Spirit of the Laws* (1748), strongly influenced his younger contemporary Rousseau and many of the American Founding Fathers, including John Adams, Jefferson, and Madison. Rejecting Aristotle's classification, Montesquieu distinguishes three ideal types of government: monarchy, "in which a single person governs by fixed and established

Portrait of the French political theorist Montesquieu. The Founding Fathers of the United States were influenced by Montesquieu's theory of the separation of powers within government. Keystone-France/Gamma Keystone/Getty Images

laws"; despotism, "in which a single person directs every-thing by his own will and caprice"; and republican (or popular) government, which may be of two types, depend-ing on whether "the body, or only a part of the people, is possessed of the supreme power," the former being a democracy, the latter an aristocracy.

According to Montesquieu, a necessary condition for the existence of a republican government, whether demo-cratic or aristocratic, is that the people in whom supreme power is lodged possess the quality of "public virtue," meaning that they are motivated by a desire to achieve the public good. Although public virtue may not be nec-essary in a monarchy and is certainly absent in despotic regimes, it must be present to some degree in aristocratic republics and to a large degree in democratic repub-lics. Sounding a theme that would be loudly echoed in Madison's "Federalist 10," Montesquieu asserts that with-out strong public virtue, a democratic republic is likely to be destroyed by conflict between various "factions," each pursuing its own narrow interests at the expense of the broader public good.

DAVID HUME

The destructive power of factions was also strongly emphasized by the Scottish philosopher and historian David Hume, whose influence on Madison was perhaps even greater than Montesquieu's. For it was from Hume that Madison seems to have acquired a view about factions that turned the issue of the desirability of larger political associations—i.e., those larger than the city-state—on its head. For the purpose of diminishing the destructive potential of factionalism, so Hume and Madison argued, bigger is in fact better, because in bigger associations each representative must look after a greater diversity of interests. It is also likely that Madison was influenced by Hume when in "Federalist 10" he rejected the term *democracy* for the type of government based on representation, preferring instead to call it a *republic*.

JEAN-JACQUES ROUSSEAU

When compared with Locke, Jean-Jacques Rousseau sometimes seems the more radical democrat, though a close reading of his work shows that, in important respects, Rousseau's conception of democracy is narrower than Locke's. Indeed, in his most influential work of political philosophy, *The Social Contract* (1762), Rousseau asserts that democracy is incompatible with representative institutions, a position that renders it all but irrelevant to nation-states. The sovereignty of the people, he argues, can be neither alienated nor represented. "The idea of representatives is modern," he wrote. "In the ancient republics ... the people never had representatives.... [T]he moment a people allows itself to be represented, it is no longer free: it no longer exists." But if representation is incompatible with democracy, and if direct democracy is the only legitimate form of government, then no nation-state of Rousseau's time or any other can have a legitimate government. Furthermore, according to Rousseau, if a political association that is small enough to practice direct democracy, such as a city-state, were to come into existence, it would inevitably be subjugated by larger nation-states and thereby cease to be democratic.

For these and other reasons, Rousseau was pessimistic about the prospects of democracy. "It is against the natural order for the many to govern and the few to be governed," he wrote. "It is unimaginable that the people should remain continually assembled to devote their time to public affairs." Adopting a view common among critics

Colour engraving of French philosopher and political theorist Jean-Jacques Rousseau. DEA/G. Dagli Orti/De Agostini/Getty Images

of democracy in his time, Rousseau also held that "there is no government so subject to civil wars and intestine agitations as democratic or popular government." In a much-cited passage, he declares that, "were there a people of gods, their government would be democratic. So perfect a government is not for men."

Despite these negative conclusions, Rousseau hints, in a brief footnote (Book III, Chapter 15), that democratic governments may be viable if joined together in confederations. Some years later, in a discussion of how the people of Poland might govern themselves, he allowed that there is simply no alternative to government by representation. However, he left the problem of the proper size or scale of democratic political associations largely unsolved.

JOHN STUART MILL

In his work *On Liberty* (1859), John Stuart Mill argued on utilitarian grounds that individual liberty cannot be legitimately infringed—whether by government, society, or individuals—except in cases where the individual's action would cause harm to others. In a celebrated formulation of this principle, Mill wrote that:

> *the sole end for which mankind are warranted, individually or collectively, in interfering with the liberty of action of any of their number, is self-protection.... The only purpose for which power can be rightfully exercised over any member of a civilised community, against his will, is to prevent harm to others. His own good, either physical or moral, is not a sufficient warrant.*

Mill's principle provided a philosophical foundation for some of the basic freedoms essential to a functioning democracy, such as freedom of association, and undermined the legitimacy of paternalistic laws, such as those requiring temperance, which in Mill's view treated adult citizens like children. In the area of what he called the liberty of thought and discussion, another freedom crucial to democracy, Mill argued, also on utilitarian grounds, that legal restrictions on the expression of opinion are never justified. The "collision of adverse opinions," he contended, is a necessary part of any society's search for the truth. In another work, *Considerations on Representative Government* (1861), Mill set forth in a lucid and penetrating manner many of the essential features of the new type of government, which had not yet emerged in Continental Europe and was still incomplete in important respects in the United States. In this work he also advanced a

UTILITARIANISM

In one common formulation, utilitarianism is the ethical theory according to which an action is right if it tends to maximize happiness, not only that of the agent but also of everyone affected. Thus, utilitarians focus on the consequences of an act rather than on its intrinsic nature or the motives of the agent. Classical utilitarianism is hedonist, but values other than, or in addition to, pleasure (ideal utilitarianism) can be employed, or—more neutrally, and in a version popular in economics— anything can be regarded as valuable that appears as an object of rational or informed desire (preference utilitarianism). The test of utility maximization can also be applied directly to single acts (act utilitarianism), or to acts only indirectly through some other suitable object of moral assessment, such as rules of conduct (rule utilitarianism). Jeremy Bentham's *Introduction to the Principles of Morals and Legislation* (1789) and John Stuart Mill's *Utilitarianism* (1863) are major statements of utilitarianism.

powerful argument on behalf of woman suffrage—a position that virtually all previous political philosophers (all of them male, of course) had ignored or rejected.

JOHN DEWEY

According to the American philosopher John Dewey, democracy is the most desirable form of government because it alone provides the kinds of freedom necessary for individual self-development and growth—including the freedom to exchange ideas and opinions with others, the freedom to form associations with others to pursue common goals, and the freedom to determine and pursue one's own conception of the good life. Democracy is more than merely a form of government, however; as Dewey remarks in *Democracy and Education* (1916), it is also a "mode of associated life" in which citizens cooperate with each other to solve their common problems through rational means (i.e., through critical inquiry and experiment) in a spirit of mutual respect and goodwill. Moreover, the political institutions of any democracy, according to Dewey, should not be viewed as the perfect and unchangeable creations of visionary statesmen of the past;

American philosopher John Dewey stressed the importance of education in a democracy. Hulton Archive/Getty Images

rather, they should be constantly subject to criticism and improvement as historical circumstances and the public interest change.

Participation in a democracy as Dewey conceived it requires critical and inquisitive habits of mind, an inclination toward cooperation with others, and a feeling of public spiritedness and a desire to achieve the common good. Because these habits and inclinations must be inculcated from a young age, Dewey placed great emphasis on education; indeed, he called public schools "the church of democracy." His contributions to both the theory and practice of education were enormously influential in the United States in the 20th century.

Dewey offered little in the way of concrete proposals regarding the form that democratic institutions should take. Nevertheless, in *The Public and Its Problems* (1927) and other works, he contended that individuals cannot develop to their fullest potential except in a social democracy, or a democratic welfare-state. Accordingly, he held that democracies should possess strong regulatory powers. He also insisted that among the most important features of a social democracy should be the right of workers to participate directly in the control of the firms in which they are employed.

Given Dewey's interest in education, it is not surprising that he was greatly concerned with the question of how citizens might better understand public affairs. Although he was a proponent of the application of the social sciences to the development of public policy, he sharply criticized intellectuals, academics, and political leaders who viewed the general public as incompetent and who often argued for some form of democratic elitism. Only the public, he maintained, can decide what the public interest is. In order for citizens to be able to make informed and responsible decisions about their common problems, he thought, it is important for them to engage in dialogue with each other in their local communities. Dewey's emphasis on dialogue as a critical practice in a democracy inspired later political theorists to explore the vital role of deliberation in democratic systems.

JÜRGEN HABERMAS

In a series of works published after 1970, the German philosopher and social theorist Jürgen Habermas, employing concepts borrowed from Anglo-American philosophy of language, argued that the idea of achieving a "rational consensus" within a group on questions of either fact or value presupposes the existence of what he called an "ideal speech situation." In such a situation, participants would be able to evaluate each other's assertions solely on the basis of reason and evidence in an atmosphere completely free of any nonrational "coercive" influences, including both physical and psychological coercion. Furthermore, all participants would be motivated solely by the desire to obtain a rational consensus, and no time limits on the discussion would be imposed. Although difficult if not impossible to realize in practice, the ideal speech situation can be used as a model of free and open public discussion and a standard against which to evaluate the practices and institutions through which large political questions and issues of public policy are decided in actual democracies.

JOHN RAWLS

From the time of Mill until about the mid-20th century, most philosophers who defended democratic principles did so largely on the basis of utilitarian considerations— i.e., they argued that systems of government that are democratic in character are more likely than other systems to produce a greater amount of happiness (or well-being) for a greater number of people. Such justifications, however, were traditionally vulnerable to the objection that they could be used to support intuitively less-desirable forms of government in which the greater happiness of the majority is achieved by unfairly neglecting the rights and interests of a minority.

In *A Theory of Justice* (1971), the American philosopher John Rawls attempted to develop a nonutilitarian justification of a democratic political order characterized by fairness, equality, and individual rights. Reviving the notion of a social contract, which had been dormant since the 18th century, he imagined a hypothetical situation in which a group of rational individuals are rendered ignorant of all social and economic facts about themselves—including facts about their race, sex, religion, education, intelligence, talents or skills, and even their conception of the "good life"—and then asked to decide what general principles should govern the political institutions under which they live. From behind this "veil of ignorance," Rawls argues, such a group would unanimously reject utilitarian principles—such as "political institutions should aim to maximize

Harvard political philosopher John Rawls. Steve Pyke/Premium Archive/ Getty Images

the happiness of the greatest number"—because no member of the group could know whether he belonged to a minority whose rights and interests might be neglected under institutions justified on utilitarian grounds.

Instead, reason and self-interest would lead the group to adopt principles such as the following: (1) everyone should have a maximum and equal degree of liberty, including all the liberties traditionally associated with democracy; (2) everyone should have an equal opportunity to seek offices and positions that offer greater rewards of wealth, power, status, or other social goods; and (3) the distribution of wealth in society should be such that those who are least well-off are better off than they would be under any other distribution, whether equal or unequal. (Rawls holds that, given certain assumptions about human motivation, some inequality in the distribution of wealth may be necessary to achieve higher levels of productivity. It is therefore possible to imagine unequal distributions of wealth in which those who are least well-off are better off than they would be under an equal distribution.) These principles amount to an egalitarian form of democratic liberalism. Rawls is accordingly regarded as the leading philosophical defender of the modern democratic capitalist welfare state.

CHAPTER 9

The Value of Democracy

Aristotle found it useful to classify actually existing governments in terms of three "ideal constitutions." For essentially the same reasons, the notion of an "ideal democracy" also can be useful for identifying and understanding the democratic characteristics of actually existing governments, be they of city-states, nation-states, or larger associations.

IDEAL DEMOCRACY

It is important to note that the term *ideal* is ambiguous. In one sense, a system is ideal if it is considered apart from, or in the absence of, certain empirical conditions, which in actuality are always present to some degree. Ideal systems in this sense are used to identify what features of an actual system are essential to it, or what underlying laws are responsible, in combination with empirical factors, for a system's behaviour in actual circumstances. In another sense, a system is ideal if it is "best" from a moral point of view. An ideal system in this sense is a goal toward which a person or society ought to strive (even if it is not perfectly attainable in practice) and a standard against which the moral worth of what has been achieved, or of what exists, can be measured.

These two senses are often confused. Systems that are ideal in the first sense may, but need not, be ideal in the second sense. Accordingly, a description of an ideal democracy, such as the one below, need not be intended to prescribe a particular political system. Indeed, influential conceptions of ideal democracy have been offered by democracy's enemies as well as by its friends.

FEATURES OF IDEAL DEMOCRACY

At a minimum, an ideal democracy would have the following features:

Effective participation. Before a policy is adopted or rejected, members of the *dēmos* have the opportunity to make their views about the policy known to other members.

Equality in voting. Members of the *dēmos* have the opportunity to vote for or against the policy, and all votes are counted as equal.

Informed electorate. Members of the *dēmos* have the opportunity, within a reasonable amount of time, to learn about the policy and about possible alternative policies and their likely consequences.

Citizen control of the agenda. The *dēmos*, and only the *dēmos*, decides what matters are placed on the decision-making agenda and how they are placed there. Thus, the democratic process is "open" in the sense that the *dēmos* can change the policies of the association at any time.

Inclusion. Each and every member of the *dēmos* is entitled to participate in the association in the ways just described.

Fundamental rights. Each of the necessary features of ideal democracy prescribes a right that is itself a necessary feature of ideal democracy: thus every member of the *dēmos* has a right to communicate with others, a right to have his voted counted equally with the votes of others, a right to gather information, a right to participate on an equal footing with other members, and a right, with other members, to exercise control of the agenda. Democracy, therefore, consists of more than just political processes; it is also necessarily a system of fundamental rights.

IDEAL AND REPRESENTATIVE DEMOCRACY

In modern representative democracies, the features of ideal democracy, to the extent that they exist, are realized through a variety of political institutions. These institutions, which are broadly similar in different countries despite significant differences in constitutional structure, were entirely new in human history at the time of their first appearance in Europe and the United States in the 18th century. Among the most important of them is, naturally, the institution of representation itself, through which all major government decisions and policies are made by popularly elected officials, who are accountable

FREEDOM OF SPEECH

In U.S. constitutional law, freedom of speech is the right, as stated in the 1st and 14th Amendments to the Constitution of the United States, to express information, ideas, and opinions free of government restrictions based on content. A modern legal test of the legitimacy of proposed restrictions on freedom of speech was stated in the opinion by U.S. Supreme Court justice Oliver Wendell Holmes, Jr., in *Schenk v. U.S.* (1919): a restriction is legitimate only if the speech in question poses a "clear and present danger"—i.e., a risk or threat to safety or to other public interests that is serious and imminent. Many cases involving freedom of speech and of the press also have concerned defamation, obscenity, and prior restraint.

to the electorate for their actions. Other important institutions include:

Free, fair, and frequent elections. Citizens may participate in
  such elections both as voters and as candidates (though
  age and residence restrictions may be imposed).
Freedom of expression. Citizens may express themselves
  publicly on a broad range of politically relevant subjects without fear of punishment.
Independent sources of information. There exist sources of
  political information that are not under the control of
  the government or any single group and whose right
  to publish or otherwise disseminate information is
  protected by law; moreover, all citizens are entitled to
  seek out and use such sources of information.

A 2010 Tea Party Express rally in Phoenix, Ariz. Within a democracy, citizens have the right to participate in independent political organizations such as the Tea Party movement. Joshua Lott/Getty Images

Freedom of association. Citizens have the right to form and to participate in independent political organizations, including parties and interest groups.

Institutions like these developed in Europe and the United States in various political and historical circumstances, and the impulses that fostered them were not always themselves democratic. Yet, as they developed, it became increasingly apparent that they were necessary for achieving a satisfactory level of democracy in any political association as large as a nation-state.

The relation between these institutions and the features of ideal democracy that are realized through them can be summarized as follows. In an association as large as a nation-state, representation is necessary for effective participation and for citizen control of the agenda; free, fair, and frequent elections are necessary for effective participation and for equality in voting; and freedom of expression, independent sources of information, and freedom of association are each necessary for effective participation, an informed electorate, and citizen control of the agenda.

ACTUAL DEMOCRACIES

Since Aristotle's time, political philosophers generally have insisted that no actual political system is likely to attain, to the fullest extent possible, all the features of its corresponding ideal. Thus, whereas the institutions of many actual systems are sufficient to attain a relatively high level of democracy, they are almost certainly not sufficient to achieve anything like perfect or ideal democracy. Nevertheless, such institutions may produce a satisfactory approximation of the ideal—as presumably they did in Athens in the 5th century BCE, when the term *democracy* was coined, and in the United States in the early 19th century, when Tocqueville, like most others in America and elsewhere, unhesitatingly called the country a democracy.

For associations that are small in population and area, the political institutions of direct democracy seem best to approximate the ideal of "government by the people." In such a democracy all matters of importance to the association as a whole can be decided on by the citizens. Citizens have the opportunity to discuss the policies that come before them and to gather information directly from those they consider well-informed, as well as from other sources. They can meet at a convenient place—the Pnyx in Athens, the Forum in Rome, the Palazzo Ducale in Venice, or the town hall in a New England village—to discuss the policy further and to offer amendments or revisions. Finally, their decision is rendered in a vote, all votes being counted equal, with the votes of a majority prevailing.

It is thus easy to see why direct democracies are sometimes thought to approach ideal democracy much more closely than representative systems ever could, and why the most ardent advocates of direct democracy have sometimes insisted, as Rousseau did in *The Social Contract*, that

Activists placing a banner supporting direct democracy on a pillar of the Bank of Greece's central headquarters, September 2011. Louisa Gouliamaki/ AFP/Getty Images

the term *representative democracy* is self-contradictory. Yet, views like these have failed to win many converts.

ADVANTAGES OF DEMOCRACY

Why should "the people" rule? Is democracy really superior to any other form of government? Although a full exploration of this issue is beyond the scope of this book, history—particularly 20th-century history—demonstrates that democracy uniquely possesses a number of features that most people, whatever their basic political beliefs, would consider desirable. Historically proven benefits are that democracy helps to prevent rule by cruel and vicious autocrats, and countries with democratic governments tend to be more prosperous than countries with nondemocratic governments. Democracy also tends to foster human development—as measured by health, education, personal income, and other indicators—more fully than other forms of government do.

Other features of democracy also would be considered desirable by most people, though some would regard them as less important than the features listed above. For instance, democracy helps people to protect their fundamental interests, and guarantees its citizens fundamental rights that nondemocratic systems do not, and cannot, grant. Democracy also ensures its citizens a broader range of personal freedoms than other forms of government do.

Finally, there are some features of democracy that some people—the critics of democracy—would not consider desirable at all, though most people, upon reflection, would regard them as at least worthwhile. Only democracy provides people with a maximum opportunity to live under laws of their own choosing, as well as a maximum opportunity to take moral responsibility for their choices and decisions about government policies. And only in a democracy can there be a relatively high level of political equality.

These advantages notwithstanding, there have been critics of democracy since ancient times. Perhaps the most enduring of their charges is that most people are incapable of participating in government in a meaningful or competent way because they lack the necessary knowledge, intelligence, wisdom, experience, or character. According to Plato, for example, the best government would be an aristocracy of "philosopher-kings" whose rigorous intellectual and moral training would make them uniquely qualified to rule. The view that the people as a whole are incapable of governing themselves has been espoused not only by kings and aristocratic rulers but also by political theorists (Plato foremost among them), religious leaders, and other authorities. The view was prevalent in one form or another throughout the world during most of recorded history until the early 20th century, and since then it has been most often invoked by opponents of democracy in Europe and elsewhere to justify various forms of dictatorship and one-party rule.

No doubt there will be critics of democracy for as long as democratic governments exist. The extent of their success in winning adherents and promoting the creation of nondemocratic regimes will depend on how well democratic governments meet the new challenges and crises that are all but certain to occur.

Conclusion

In a world increasingly knit together by international trade and global communications and information technology, the future of the nation-state is uncertain. It seems ever more unlikely that national governments, acting independently or in groups, can on their own successfully handle the universal enemies of poverty, hunger, disease, environmental degradation, terrorism, and war. Some thinkers believe that only a form of world government can make decisive headway against those evils, but no one has yet suggested convincingly either how a world government could be set up without another world war or how, if such a government did somehow come peacefully into existence, it could be organized so as to be worthy of its name. Even effective global cooperation among national governments can be extremely difficult, as the examples of the United Nations and other international bodies have shown. Nevertheless, those bodies have had many accomplishments, the European Union (EU) being particularly successful.

Democracy in particular is threatened in many non-Western countries by poverty, unemployment, inflation, corruption, and massive inequalities in income and wealth. The absence of a large middle class and limited educational opportunities for ordinary citizens have impeded the development of democratic political culture in some countries, as have the lack of an effective legal system and the division of the population into antagonistic ethnic, racial, or religious groups. Even in some developed countries the political culture, for various reasons, does not sufficiently inculcate in citizens the kinds of beliefs and values that tend to support democratic institutions and practices in times of crisis or even during the ordinary conflicts of political life.

In all democratic and near-democratic countries, nationalism still distorts voters' judgments in matters of foreign policy, as greed misleads them in economic policy. Class conflicts have been muted rather than resolved. Demagogues abound as much as they did in ancient Athens. Just as the incompatible claims of the city-states ruined ancient Greece and undermined Athenian democracy, so the rival claims of the nation-states may yet imperil modern civilization. At least one thing is clear, however. If human beings, as political animals, are to progress further, they cannot yet rest from seeking new forms of government to meet the ever-changing needs of their times.

anarchy A state of lawlessness or political disorder due to the absence of governmental authority.

authoritarian Of, relating to, or favouring a concentration of power in a leader or an elite not constitutionally responsible to the people.

autonomy The quality or state of being self-governing.

bicameral Having, consisting of, or based on two legislative chambers.

bureaucracy A body of nonelective government officials.

canton Small territorial or political subdivision within France, Switzerland and other European countries.

capitalism An economic system characterized by private ownership of the means of production, and in which prices, production, and the distribution of goods and income are determined mainly by competition in a free market.

consul Either of two annually elected chief magistrates of the Roman republic.

demagogue A leader who makes use of popular prejudices and false claims and promises in order to gain power.

democracy A government in which the supreme power is vested in the people and exercised by them directly or indirectly through a system of representation usually involving periodically held free elections.

federate To form an encompassing political or societal entity by uniting smaller or more localized entities.

feudalism The system of political organization characterized by homage of vassals to a lord, wherein all land held in fee and service is expected of tenants under arms and in court.

liberalism Political doctrine that takes protecting and enhancing the freedom of the individual to be the central problem of politics.

monarchy Undivided rule or absolute sovereignty by a single person.

oligarchy A government in which a small group exercises control, especially for corrupt and selfish purposes.

potentate One who wields great power or sway.

proletariat The class of industrial workers who lack their own means of production and hence sell their labour to live.

republic A government in which supreme power resides in a body of citizens entitled to vote and is exercised by elected officers and representatives responsible to them and governing according to law.

shogun One of a line of military governors ruling Japan until the revolution of 1867–68.

sinecure An office or position that requires little or no work and that usually provides an income.

socialism A social and economic doctrine that calls for public rather than private ownership or control of property and natural resources.

timocracy Government in which a certain amount of property is necessary for office.

totalitarianism Centralized control by an autocratic authority.

utilitarianism A theory that the aim of action should be the largest possible balance of pleasure over pain or the greatest happiness of the greatest number.

GOVERNMENT

The study of government requires a solid background in world history, and William H. McNeill, *A World History*, 4th ed. (1999), is an excellent introduction. The development of governmental forms in Greece can be found in *The Cambridge Ancient History*, 3rd ed. (1970–2000); and in N.G.L. Hammond, *A History of Greece to 322 B.C.*, 3rd ed. (1986). Those wanting general accounts of the Romans may turn to H.H. Scullard, *From the Gracchi to Nero: A History of Rome from 133 B.C. to A.D. 68*, 5th ed. (1982, reprinted 1992). A.H.M. Jones, *The Later Roman Empire, 284–602: A Social, Economic, and Administrative Survey*, 2 vol. (1964, reprinted 1986), is the most authoritative account of the fall of the empire.

Marc Bloch, *Feudal Society* (1961, reprinted 1989; originally published in French, 1939), is an indispensable study of its subject.

The development of political thought from the Renaissance to the 19th century is well presented in John Plamenatz, *Man and Society: Political and Social Theories from Machiavelli to Marx*, new 2nd ed., rev. by M.E. Plamenatz and Robert Wokler, 3 vol. (1992).

Useful studies of English government include J.H. Plumb, *The Growth of Political Stability in England, 1675–1725* (1967, reissued 1980); and Elie Halevy, *A History of the English People in the Nineteenth Century*, 2nd rev. ed., 6 vol. in 7, trans. from French (1949–52). The French experience is dealt with in C.B.A. Behrens, *The Ancien*

Régime (1967, reissued 1989); Georges Lefebvre, _The French Revolution_, 2 vol. (1962–64; originally published in French, 1930); and D.W. Brogan, _The French Nation from Napoleon to Pétain, 1814–1940_ (1957, reissued 1989). Prussia and the development of fascist Germany are discussed in Hans Rosenberg, _Bureaucracy, Aristocracy, and Autocracy: The Prussian Experience, 1660–1815_ (1958, reissued 1968); and A.J. Nicholls, _Weimar and the Rise of Hitler_, 4th ed. (2000). A good source on Italy is Denis Mack Smith, _Italy: A Modern History_, new ed. rev. and enlarged (1969). Jerome Blum, _Lord and Peasant in Russia: From the Ninth to the Nineteenth Century_ (1961, reissued 1971); and Ronald Grigor Suny, _The Soviet Experiment: Russia, the U.S.S.R., and the Successor States_ (1998), deal with Russia and the Soviet Union. Coverage of the United States is provided in Richard Hofstadter, _The American Political Tradition and the Men Who Made It_ (1948, reissued 1996); and Melvyn Dubofsky and Athan Theoharis, _Imperial Democracy: The United States Since 1945_ (1988).

DEMOCRACY

A concise introduction is Alan F. Hattersley, _A Short History of Democracy_ (1930). Historical and theoretical approaches are combined in John Dunn (ed.), _Democracy: The Unfinished Journey, 508 BC to AD 1993_ (1992, reprinted with corrections 1993); and Sanford Lakoff, _Democracy: History, Theory, and Practice_ (1996).

Index